To Matt,

Love Mom & Dad.
Dec 2010.

D0028591

Things I Wish I'd Known Before We Got Married

Things I Wish I'd Known Before We Got Married

GARY D. CHAPMAN, PhD

NORTHFIELD PUBLISHING
CHICAGO

© 2010 BY
GARY D. CHAPMAN

All rights reserved. No part of this book may be reproduced in any form without permission in writing from the publisher, except in the case of brief quotations embodied in critical articles or reviews.

All Scripture quotations, unless otherwise indicated, are taken from the *Holy Bible, New International Version*®, NIV®. Copyright© 1973, 1978, 1984 by Biblica, Inc.™ Used by permission of Zondervan. All rights reserved worldwide.

Scripture quotations marked (TNIV) are taken from the *Holy Bible, Today's New International Version*®. TNIV®. Copyright© 2001, 2005 by Biblica, Inc.™ Used by permission of Zondervan. All rights reserved worldwide.

All websites listed herein are accurate at the time of publication, but may change in the future or cease to exist. The listing of website references and resources does not imply publisher endorsement of the site's entire contents. Groups, corporations, and organizations are listed for informational purposes, and listing does not imply publisher endorsement of their activities.

Edited by Elizabeth Cody Newenhuyse
Cover design: Faceout Studios
Interior design: Smartt Guys design
Author Photo: Alysia Grimes Photography

Library of Congress Cataloging-in-Publication Data

Chapman, Gary D.
Things I wish I'd known before we got married / Gary D. Chapman.
p. cm.
ISBN 978-0-8024-8183-2
1. Marriage. 2. Communication in marriage. 3. Marriage--Religious aspects--Christianity. I. Title.
HQ734.C4678 2010
248.8'44--dc22

2010013313

Moody Publishers is committed to caring wisely for God's creation and uses recycled paper whenever possible. The paper in this book consists of 10 percent post-consumer waste.

We hope you enjoy this book from Northfield Publishing. Our goal is to provide high-quality, thought-provoking books and products that connect truth to your real needs and challenges. For more information on other books and products written and produced from a biblical perspective, go to www.moodypublishers.com or write to:

Northfield Publishing
820 N. LaSalle Boulevard
Chicago, IL 60610

1 3 5 7 9 10 8 6 4 2

Printed in the United States of America

Other Books by Gary Chapman

The Five Love Languages

The Five Love Languages Men's Edition

The Five Love Languages Gift Edition

The Five Love Languages of Children

The Five Love Languages of Teenagers

The Five Love Languages Singles Edition

The Five Languages of Apology

God Speaks Your Love Language

The Marriage You've Always Wanted

The Marriage You've Always Wanted Bible Study

The Family You've Always Wanted

Hope for the Separated

Parenting Your Adult Child

Desperate Marriages

Anger

CONTENTS

Introduction

In my undergraduate studies, my academic major was anthropology. Later, I completed a master's degree in the same field. For over forty years, I have continued to study human cultures. One conclusion is inevitable. Marriage, between a man and woman, is the foundation of all human societies. The reality is that when children become adults, most of them will get married. In the United States, each year there are over two million marriages; that is four million people who are saying "I do" to the question, "Will you have this man to be your wedded husband?" or "Will you have this woman to be your wedded wife?" Almost all these couples anticipate "living happily ever after." No one gets married hoping to be miserable or to make their spouse miserable. Yet we all know that the divorce rate in Western cultures continues to hover around fifty percent, and the highest percentage of divorces occur within the first seven years of marriage.

People do not get married planning to divorce. Divorce is the result of a lack of preparation for marriage and the failure to learn the skills of working together as teammates in an intimate relationship. What is ironic is that we recognize the need for education in all other pursuits of life and fail to recognize that need when it comes to marriage. Most people spend far more time in preparation for their vocation than they do in preparation for marriage. Therefore, it should not be surprising that they are more successful in their vocational pursuits than they are in reaching the goal of marital happiness.

This is not a book on how to plan a wedding. This is a book on how to have a successful marriage.

The decision to get married will impact one's life more deeply than almost any decision in life. Yet people continue to rush into marriage with little or no preparation for making a marriage successful. In fact, many couples give far more attention to making plans for the wedding than making plans for marriage. The wedding festivities last only a few hours, while the marriage, we hope, will last for a lifetime.

This is not a book on how to plan a wedding. This is a book on how to have a successful marriage. I've spent the last thirty-five years of my life counseling with couples whose dreams of a happy marriage have been shattered in the real world of dirty dishes, unpaid bills, conflicting work schedules, and crying babies. With hard work and months of counseling, many of these couples have gone on to have good marriages. For that, I am grateful.

It is my conviction that many of these struggles could have been avoided had the couple taken time to prepare more thoroughly for marriage. That is why I am writing this book. I want you to learn from their mistakes. It is much less painful than learning from your own mistakes. I want you to have the kind of loving, supportive, mutually beneficial marriage that you envision. However, I can assure you, that kind of marriage will not happen simply because you get married. You must make time to discover and practice the proven marital guidelines that make such a marriage possible.

For the individual who is not in a dating relationship and has no immediate prospects of marriage, the book will provide a blueprint on moving from singleness to marriage. For the couple who is dating but not yet engaged, it will help you decide if and when to announce your plans to get married. For the engaged couple, it will help you examine the foundation and learn the skills that are necessary for building a successful marriage.

As I look back over the early years of my marriage, I wish someone had told me what I am about to tell you. I honestly think I would have listened. However, in my generation, the concept of "preparation for marriage" did not exist. I'm hoping that my openness about my own marriage will help you avoid some of the pain and frustration that Karolyn and I experienced.

This is not a book simply to be read. It is a book to be experienced. The more you grapple with the realities discussed in the following pages and share honestly your thoughts and feelings on these topics, respect each other's opinions and find workable solutions to your differences, to that degree you will be prepared for marriage. To the degree that you ignore these issues and choose to believe that the euphoric feelings that you have for each other will carry you through, you set yourself up for failure. It is my desire that you will prepare for your marriage as though it were the most important human relationship you will ever have. If you give it your full and best attention, you will be on the road to seeing your dreams of marital happiness come true.

I'd like to invite you to visit Startmarriageright.com where you'll find a variety of helpful resources both for preparing for marriage and building a successful, lifelong marriage. Most of these resources are free so, I hope that you'll check it out. And, remember, your wedding day is just the beginning!

–Gary Chapman

1

I Wish I Had Known . . .

That being in love is not an ADEQUATE FOUNDATION *for building a* SUCCESSFUL MARRIAGE

It should have been obvious, but I missed it. I had never read a book on marriage so my mind was not cluttered with reality. I just knew that I had feelings for Karolyn that I had never felt with any other girl. When we kissed, it was like a trip to heaven. When I saw her after an extended absence, I actually felt chill bumps. I liked everything about her. I liked the way she looked, the way she talked, the way she walked, and I was especially captivated by her brown eyes. I even liked her mother and volunteered to paint her house—anything to let this girl know how much I loved her. I could not imagine any other girl being more wonderful than she. I think she had the same thoughts and feelings about me.

With all of these thoughts and feelings, we fully intended

to make each other happy the rest of our lives. Yet, within six months after marriage, we were both more miserable than we had ever imagined. The euphoric feelings were gone, and instead, we felt hurt, anger, disappointment, and resentment. This, we never anticipated when we were "in love." We thought that the positive perceptions and feelings we had for each other would be with us for a lifetime.

Over the past thirty years, I have done premarital counseling sessions with hundreds of couples. I have found that most of them have the same limited perspective about being in love. I have often asked couples in our first session this question: "Why do you want to get married?" Whatever else they say, they always give me the big reason. And the big reason is almost always the same: "Because we love each other." Then I ask a very unfair question: "What do you mean by that?" Typically they are stunned by the question. Most say something about a deep feeling that they have for each other. It has persisted for some time and is in some way different from what they have felt for other dating partners. Often they look at each other, they look at the ceiling, they giggle, and then one of them says, "Well, ahh . . . oh, you know." At this stage of my life, I think I do know—but I doubt that they know. I fear that they have the same perception of being in love that Karolyn and I had when we got married. And I know now that being in love is not a sufficient foundation on which to build a successful marriage.

Some time ago I had a call from a young man who asked if I would perform his wedding ceremony. I inquired as to when he wanted to get married and found that the wedding date was less than a week away. I explained that I usually have from six to eight counseling sessions with those who desire to be married.

His response was classic: "Well, to be honest with you, I don't think we need any counseling. We really love each other and I don't think we will have any problems." I smiled and then wept inwardly—another victim of the "in love" illusion.

We often speak of "falling in love." When I hear this phrase, I am reminded of the jungle animal hunt. A hole is dug in the midst of the animal's path to the water hole, then camouflaged with branches and leaves. The poor animal runs along, minding his own business. Then all of a sudden it falls into the pit and is trapped.

This is the manner in which we speak of love. We are walking along doing our normal duties when all of a sudden, we look across the room or down the hall, and there she/he is—wham-o, "we fall in love." There is nothing we can do about it. It is completely beyond our control. We know we are destined for marriage; the sooner the better. So, we tell our friends and because they operate on the same principle, they agree that if we are really in love, then it is time for marriage.

Often we fail to consider the fact that our social, spiritual, and intellectual interests are miles apart. Our value systems and goals are contradictory, but we are in love. The great tragedy stemming from this perception of love is that a year after the marriage, a couple sits in the counselor's office and say, "We don't love each other anymore." Therefore, they are ready to separate. After all, if "love" is gone, then "surely you don't expect us to stay together."

When "the Tingles" Strike

I have a different word for the above-described emotional experience. I call it "the tingles." We get warm, bubbly, tingly feelings for a member of the opposite sex. It is the tingles that motivate us to go out for a hamburger with him/her. Sometimes we lose the tingles on the first date. We find out something about them that simply shuts our emotions down. The next time they invite us for a hamburger, we are not hungry. However, in other relationships, the more we are together, the tinglier the feeling. Before long, we find ourselves thinking about them day and night. Our thoughts are obsessive in nature. We see them as the most wonderful, exciting person we have ever known. We want to be together every possible moment. We dream of sharing the rest of our lives making each other happy.

Please do not misunderstand me. I think the tingles are important. They are real, and I am in favor of their survival. But they are not the basis for a satisfactory marriage. I am not suggesting that one should marry without the tingles. Those warm, excited feelings, the chill bumps, that sense of acceptance, the excitement of the touch that make up the tingles serve as the cherry on top of the sundae. But you cannot have a sundae with only the cherry. The many other factors that we discuss in this book must be a vital consideration in making a decision about marriage.

Being in love is an emotional and obsessive experience. However, emotions change and obsessions fade. Research indicates that the average life span of the "in love" obsession is two years.[1] For some it may last a bit longer; for some, a bit less. But the average is two years. Then we come down off the emotional high and those aspects of life that we disregarded in our euphoria begin to become important. Our differences begin to emerge and we often find ourselves arguing with the person whom we once thought to be perfect. We have now discovered for ourselves that being in love is not the foundation for a happy marriage.

For those of you who are currently in a dating relationship and are perhaps contemplating marriage, I would encourage you to read the Appendix of this book, located on page 149. I believe that the primary purpose of dating is to get to know each other and to examine the intellectual, emotional, social, spiritual, and physical foundations for marriage. Only then are you able to make a wise decision—to marry or not to marry. The questions contained in the learning exercises in the Appendix will assist you in discussing these foundations.

Talking It Over

1. On a scale of 0–10, how strongly do you feel the "tingles" for the person you are dating?
2. If the average "life span" of the tingles is two years, how much longer can you expect to have the euphoric feelings?
3. To what degree have you explored the more important issues of compatibility in the following areas?

   — intellectual dialogue

   — emotional control

   — social interests

   — spiritual unity

   — common values
4. If you would like to explore these areas more fully, you may wish to use the questions found in the appendix, "Developing A Healthy Dating Relationship" on pages 149–161.

2

I Wish I Had Known . . .

That ROMANTIC LOVE *has two* STAGES

I was in the airport in Chicago when I met Jan, who was on her way to visit her fiancé for the weekend. When she inquired about where I was going, I said, "I'm going to Milwaukee, Wisconsin, to lead a marriage seminar tomorrow." "What do you do at marriage seminars?" she asked. "I try to give people practical ideas on how to work on their marriage," I replied. With a question in her eyes she asked, "Why do you have to work on a marriage? If you love each other, isn't that all that matters?" I knew she was sincere because that was also my perception before I got married.

With a question in her eyes she asked, "Why do you have to work on a marriage?"

Since neither of us was rushed for our next flight, I took time to explain to her that there are two stages of romantic love. The first stage requires little effort. We are pushed along by euphoric feelings (which I described in the previous chapter). We commonly call this stage "being in love." When we are *in love,* we freely do things for each other without thought of cost or sacrifice. We will drive 500 miles or fly halfway across the country in order to spend a weekend together. Jan nodded approval. The person we love seems to be perfect—at least perfect for us. I quickly added, "Now, your mother may have a different opinion. She may say, 'Honey, have you considered . . .'" Jan smiled and said, "Yes, I've heard that lecture."

In this stage of romantic love, the couple does not have to *work* on the relationship. They may expend great energy in doing things for each other, but they would not consider it work. They would tend to use the word *delight.* They feel elated with the opportunity to do something meaningful for the other person. They want to make each other happy and they often do. However, as I indicated in Chapter One, the average life span of this initial stage of romantic love is two years. We do not stay in the euphoric stage of love forever. Actually, this is good because it is difficult to concentrate on anything else when you are *in love.* If you are in college when you fall in love, your grades will likely decline. Tomorrow you have a test on the War of 1812. Who cares about the War of 1812 when you are in love? Education seems trivial; what matters is being with the person you love. All of us have known individuals who drop out of college and choose to get married because the one they love is moving to a different state and they want to go with them.

If the obsessive nature of the *in love* euphoria extended for the next twenty years, few of us would accomplish our educational and vocational potential. Involvement in social issues and philanthropic endeavors would be nil. When we are *in love*, the rest of the world doesn't matter. We are totally focused on being with each other and making each other happy.

Before I got married, no one informed me that there were two stages of romantic love. I knew that I was in love with Karolyn and I anticipated having these feelings toward her for the rest of my life. I knew that she made me happy, and I wanted to do the same for her. When in fact I came down off of the emotional high, I was disillusioned. I remembered the warnings my mother had given me, and I was plagued with the recurring thought, "I have married the wrong person." I reasoned that if I had married the right person, surely my feelings would not have subsided so quickly after marriage. These were painful thoughts that were hard to shake. *Our differences seem so obvious now. Why did I not see them earlier?*

The second stage of romantic love is much more intentional than the first stage.

The Second Stage of Love

I wish someone had been there to tell me that what I was thinking and feeling was normal; that in fact, there are two stages to romantic love and I had to make the transition. Unfortunately, no one was there to give me this information. Had I received the information I am about to give to you, it would have saved me from years of marital struggle. What I have discovered is that the second stage of romantic love is much more intentional than the first stage. And, yes, it requires work in order to keep emotional love alive. However, for those who make the effort to transition from Stage One to Stage Two, the rewards are astounding.

As a young marriage counselor, I began to discover that what makes one person feel loved does not necessarily make another person feel loved; and that when couples come down off the *in love* emotional high, they often miss each other in their efforts to express love. She says, "I feel like he doesn't love me," and he says, "I don't understand that. I work hard. I keep the car clean. I mow the grass every weekend. I help her around the house. I don't know what else she would want." She responds, "He does all those things. He is a hardworking man." Then with tears in her eyes she says, "But we don't ever talk."

Week after week, I kept hearing similar stories. So I decided to look at the notes I had made when I was counseling couples and ask myself, "When someone said, 'I feel like my spouse doesn't love me,' what were they looking for? What did they want? What were they complaining about?" Their complaints fell into five categories. I later called them the five love languages.

The dynamics are very similar to spoken languages. Each of us grows up speaking a language with a dialect. I grew up speaking English Southern-style. But everyone has a language and a dialect and that is the one we understand best. The same is true with love. Everyone has a primary love language. One of the five speaks more deeply to us emotionally than the other four. I also discovered that seldom do a husband and wife have the same love language. By nature we tend to speak our own language. Whatever makes us feel loved is what we do for the other person. But if it is not his/her language, it will not mean to them what it means to us. In the illustration above, the husband was speaking the language of *acts of service.* He was washing the car, mowing the grass, helping her around the house. To him, this is the way you express love. But her love language was *quality time.* She said, "We don't ever talk." What made her feel loved was him giving her his undivided attention talking, sharing life, listening, and communicating. He was sincerely expressing love but it was not in her primary love language.

The book that grew out of this research is entitled *The Five Love Languages: The Secret to Love that Lasts.* It has sold over six million copies in English and has been translated into thirty-eight languages around the world. It has helped literally millions of couples learn how to connect with each other and keep emotional love alive. They have made the transition from Stage One to Stage Two. They have learned how to express love effectively.

Here is a brief summary of the five love languages:

1. **Words of Affirmation.** This language uses words to affirm the other person. "I really appreciate your washing the car. It looks great." "Thanks for taking out the garbage. You are the greatest." "You look nice in that outfit." "I love the fact that you are so optimistic." "I admire the way you helped your mother." "Your smile is contagious. Did you see the way everyone seemed to brighten up when you came into the room?" All of these are words of affirmation. Your words may focus on the other person's personality or the way they look or something they have done for you or for others. To speak this language, you look for things you admire or appreciate about the person and you verbally express your admiration. If a person's primary love language is *words of affirmation,* your words will be like rain falling on dry soil. Nothing will speak more deeply of your love than words of affirmation.

2. **Acts of Service.** For these people, actions speak louder than words. If you speak words of affirmation to this person such as "I admire you, I appreciate you, I love you," they will likely think and perhaps say, "If you love me, why don't you do something to help me around the house?" If *acts of service* is their primary love language, then washing the car, mowing the grass, helping around the house, and changing the baby's diaper is precisely what makes them feel loved. The key to loving this person is to find out what things they would like for you to do. Then do them consistently.
3. **Receiving Gifts.** For some people, what makes them feel most loved is to receive a gift. The gift communicates, "He was thinking about me. Look what he got for me." The best gifts are those that you know will be appreciated. To give her a fishing rod when she does not enjoy fishing will probably not communicate your love very well. How do you find out what the other person would like to receive? You ask questions and you make observations. You observe the comments they make when they receive gifts from other family members. Listen carefully and you will discover the kind of gifts they appreciate most. Also listen to the comments they make when they are looking through a shopping catalog or watching QVC. If they say, "I'd like to have one of those," make a note of it. You can also overtly ask, "If I wanted to give you a gift, give me a list of things you would like to have." Better to give a gift that they have requested than to surprise them with a gift they do not desire. Not all gifts need to be expensive. A rose, a candy bar, a card, a book—any of these can communicate love deeply to the person whose love language is *receiving gifts.*

4. **Quality Time.** Quality time is giving the other person your undivided attention. It is not sitting in the same room watching television. Someone else has your attention. It is being in the same room with the TV off, the magazine on the table, looking at each other, talking and listening. It may also be taking a walk together so long as your purpose is to be with each other, not simply to get exercise. Couples who go to a restaurant and never talk to each other have not spoken the language of *quality time.* They have simply met their physical need for food. Quality time says, "I'm doing this because I want to be with you." Whether you are planting a garden together or going on a camping trip, the ultimate purpose is to spend time with each other. For some people, nothing makes them feel more loved than *quality time.*
5. **Physical Touch.** We have long known the emotional power of physical touch. Research indicates that babies who are touched and cuddled fare better emotionally than babies who spend long periods of time without physical touch. Every culture has appropriate and inappropriate touches between members of the opposite of sex. Appropriate touch is loving. Inappropriate touch is demeaning. To the person whose primary love language is *physical touch,* nothing speaks more deeply than appropriate touch.

How to Find Your Love Language

Here are three approaches to help you discover your own primary love language. First, *observe your own behavior.* How do you typically express love and appreciation to other people? If you are always patting people on the back or giving them hugs, then your primary language may be *physical touch*. If you freely give encouraging words to others, then *words of affirmation* is likely your love language. If you are a gift giver, then perhaps what you desire is *receiving gifts*. If you enjoy having lunch or taking a walk with a friend, then *quality time* is probably your love language. If you are always looking for ways to help people, then *acts of service* may well be your love language. The language you speak is most likely the language you wish to receive.

Second, *what do you complain about?* In any human relationship, what is your most common complaint? If you often complain that people don't help you, then *acts of service* is likely your language. If you say to a friend, "We don't ever spend time together," then you are requesting *quality time*. If your friend goes on a business trip and you say, "You didn't bring me anything?" you are revealing that *receiving gifts* is your primary love language. If you say, "I don't think you would ever touch me if I didn't initiate it," you are saying that *physical touch* is your love language. If you complain, "I don't ever do anything right," your complaint indicates that *words of affirmation* speak deeply to you. The complaints reveal what you most like to receive from other people.

Third, *what do you request most often?* If your friend is leaving on a business trip and you say, "Be sure and bring me a surprise," you are indicating that gifts are important to you. If you say, "Could we take a walk together this evening?" you are requesting *quality time*. If you ask for a back rub, you are revealing that *physical touch* speaks deeply to you. If you often ask people to do things to help you, *acts of service* is likely your love language. When you ask, "Did I do a good job?" you are requesting *words of affirmation.*

Observe how you most often express love and appreciation to others; list your complaints and requests, and you will likely be able to determine your own primary love language. Have your friend answer the same three questions and they can discover their love language. You may also wish to take the free love language quiz available at www.5lovelanguages.com.

It will be obvious that learning to speak a love language other than your own will take effort. The person who did not grow up receiving words of affirmation may find it difficult to give them. The person who grew up in a family that was not "touchy-feely" will have to learn to speak the language of physical touch. The good news is that all of these languages can be learned and the more you speak them, the easier they become.

My wife's love language is *acts of service*. That's why I vacuum floors, wash dishes, and take out the garbage. It's a small price to keep love alive. My language is *words of affirmation*. That's why I never leave the house without hearing my wife give me a positive word. Without hesitation, I can say that the emotional depth of our love for each other is far deeper than in those early days when we were swept along by euphoric feelings. Keeping romantic love alive in a marriage requires making a successful transition from Stage One to Stage Two. Learning each other's primary love language while you are dating will make the transition much easier. That is my desire for you.

Talking It Over

1. What do you think is your primary love language? Why?
2. If you are dating, what do you think is the primary love language of your partner?
3. Perhaps you would like to take the love languages quiz found at 5lovelanguages.com.
4. Discuss how you think this information will enhance your relationship.
5. If you have not read *The Five Love Languages Singles Edition*, you may wish to read it together and discuss its implications in all of your relationships.

3

I Wish I Had Known . . .

That the saying **"LIKE MOTHER, LIKE DAUGHTER"** *and* **"LIKE FATHER, LIKE SON"** *is not a myth*

I am not suggesting that the girl you marry will turn out to be exactly like her mother, nor that the man will be exactly like his father. I am saying that you are both greatly influenced by your parents.

If he has a father who is controlling and verbally abusive, don't be surprised if in ten years he has similar traits. To some degree, we are all products of our environment. Research indicates that abusive men were almost always abused as children.[1]

You may be asking, "But can't we learn from their poor example and change our own behavior?" The answer is yes, and the important word is "learn." If the son of an abuser does not take specific steps to understand abuse—why his father became an abuser, and what he needs to do to break the pattern—then he is likely to repeat it.

If a girl's mother is alcoholic, we know that statistically she is more likely to become an alcoholic.[2] However, she is not *destined* to alcoholism. If she takes positive action to understand alcoholism and learns more constructive ways to respond to stress and disappointment, she can break the alcoholic chain. Therefore, in a dating relationship if either of you has a parent with a destructive lifestyle, the responsible action is to enroll in a class, read books, talk with counselors, and discuss with each other what you are learning. Don't sweep these issues under the rug.

On the lighter side, look at the physical appearance of your same-sex parent and you are likely looking at yourself twenty years from now. If the father is balding, the son may well look the same in twenty years. If the mother is active and energetic, so will the daughter be.

Recently, my wife and I spent a week at the beach with our daughter Shelley, her husband John, and our two grandchildren. After breakfast the first morning, we carried our umbrella to the beach. Our son-in-law was on one knee and, with an auger, was boring a hole into the ground so that we could set up the umbrella. With a smile on her face, our daughter dipped her hand in a bucket of water and sprinkled the cold water on her husband's back. I said to her, "You are illustrating one of the points in my book—'like mother, like daughter.' That's exactly the kind of thing your mother would do." Later that day as John was leaving to go to the grocery store, Shelley said to us, loud enough for John to hear, "He's such a wonderful husband." That too is what her mother has said of me on numerous occasions. While I don't

Most of us are far more like our parents than we realize.

know about the truthfulness of the statement, I must confess I like to hear it. I have an idea that John feels the same way.

Whether we are talking about positive or negative characteristics, most of us are far more like our parents than we realize. I remember the young husband who said to me, "I knew that her mother did not wear makeup. She was the product of the 'hippie generation.' But I never dreamed that Julia would decide to stop wearing makeup. As long as I've known her, she's worn makeup. We never discussed it while we were dating because I never thought it would be a problem. But now we are having these long discussions about the pros and cons of makeup. I don't think I'm going to win the argument."

Communication patterns are another area in which we tend to be like our parents. For example, if you notice that her mother often interrupts her father when he is talking and corrects the details of his story by saying such things as "No, it wasn't on Tuesday, it was on Wednesday" or "It wasn't 2005, it was 2006," then you can expect the daughter to do the same. Perhaps you have already observed this behavior when you are talking. If this irritates you, now is the time to talk about it. If this pattern is not changed before marriage, it will not automatically change when you do get married.

"Her mother talks constantly. I feel trapped when I'm in her presence."

One young man said, "It scares me to death when I am around her parents. Her mother talks constantly. She hardly takes a breath between sentences. She tells these elaborate stories, giving all the details. I feel trapped when I'm in her presence. There's no good place to leave the room to get a drink of water. I see a little bit of this in Annie and I'm afraid she's going to become like her mother. I don't think I can handle that." I was thrilled to hear him express this concern while they were still dating. I could tell that Annie did not quite understand what he was saying. So I suggested that the next time he was in the presence of his mother-in-law, he simply record thirty minutes of the conversation.

Later, when Annie listened to this recording, she realized that her mother seldom asked questions and when she did, she gave the other person only a moment to answer before she jumped back into her flow of words. She now understood how this speech pattern could not only be offensive but actually stifle genuine dialogue.

Because we have grown up with our parents, we don't recognize their patterns of communication as being unhealthy. For us, it is simply the way it has always been. It often takes someone outside the family drawing the communication pattern to our attention to help us understand why the pattern needs to be changed. Because we are influenced by our parents' communication patterns, we are very likely to adopt them as our own. The good news is that these communication patterns can be changed and the time to make the change is while you are dating.

If you observe his mom and dad arguing and you notice that his father eventually walks out of the room and leaves his wife's last statement hanging in the air, then you can expect that is the way the man you are dating will likely respond to arguments after you get married. Unless, of course, he reads this book and the two of you find a healthier way to resolve your conflicts.

Also look at the common courtesies that your mom and dad extend to each other. Does her father open the car door for her mother? If so, this is what she will expect of you. Does his father remove his ball cap when he enters the house? If not, that is what you can expect of his son. Do you hear her mother answering for her father before he has the chance to speak? If so, that's what you can expect of her daughter. Does his father look at his wife when she is talking to him or does he watch television and give her no response? Whatever he does is likely what his son will do. Does her mother continually nag her father about cleaning up the garage or some other task that she wants him to do? If so, you can expect that from her daughter.

Is his father quiet and reserved or loud and outspoken? Is her mother independent, making her own decisions and seldom conferring with her husband? Does her mother cook meals? Does his father keep the car clean? Is her mother a stay-at-home mom or does she have her own vocation? Does his father own his own business or does he work for a company? Does his father mow the grass or does he hire someone to do it? Does her mother keep scrapbooks and photo albums? Is her mother highly active in church activities? What about his father? The answers to these questions will tell you what you can expect if you marry the person you are now dating. If any of the answers to these questions disturb you, this is the time to discuss them openly. The solution lies either in accepting these traits or negotiating change.

Often in today's fast-moving culture, dating couples will spend little time with each other's parents. They come to marriage without any clear understanding of the parental model with which the other person grew up. Even when couples spend time with each other's parents, they are not closely observing the behavior and communication patterns of parents. They may express appreciation for the positive things that they observe but are likely to ignore negative patterns of speech or behavior—because they cannot imagine that the person they are dating would ever adopt those negative behaviors.

What I am saying is that they are, in fact, most likely to adopt those behaviors—unless conscious attention is given and positive steps taken to keep the young adult from drifting into the patterns they observed in childhood.

This is why I encourage couples to have enough exposure to each other's parents to get to know their personalities, communication patterns, values, and especially how they relate to each other. This is the model that has greatly influenced the person you are dating. If you observe things that trouble you, these need to be discussed thoroughly with your dating partner. If your concerns are serious, you need to discuss what steps will be taken to make sure that the old sayings "Like mother, like daughter" and "Like father, like son" will not become a reality in your relationship.

Talking It Over

For the man:

1. Make a list of the things you like about your father. Then make a list of the things you consider to be negative traits in your father. If the girl you are dating has spent considerable time with your father, ask her to make similar lists about observations she has made about your father.

2. Use these lists as a basis for discussing the ways in which you would like to be different from your father.

3. What specific steps will you take to begin to make these changes?

For the woman:

1. Make a list of the things you like about your mother. Then make a list of the things you consider to be negative traits in your mother. If the man you are dating has spent considerable time with your mother, ask him to make similar lists about observations he has made about your mother.
2. Use these lists as a basis for discussing the ways in which you would like to be different from your mother.
3. What specific steps will you take to begin to make these changes?

4

I Wish I Had Known . . .

How to solve DISAGREEMENTS *without* ARGUING

When we were dating, it never crossed my mind that we would have any major disagreements. We seemed so compatible. I was willing to do whatever she desired, and she seemed to be willing to follow my suggestions. That was one of the things that attracted me to her. To think that we would ever end up arguing with each other never occurred to me.

However, starting on the honeymoon and continuing for the first few years of our marriage, we found ourselves embroiled in conflicts. I could not imagine how illogical she was and she could not imagine that I could be so harsh and demanding. It was not that I wanted to be harsh; it's just that I knew that my idea was the best idea. Of course, she felt the same way about her ideas. No one had ever told us that conflicts are a normal part of every

> I knew that my idea was the best idea. Of course, she felt the same way about her ideas.

marriage. There are no married couples who do not encounter conflicts, for one simple reason—we are individuals. As individuals we have different desires, different likes and dislikes, different things that irritate and please us. For example, I discovered that Karolyn liked to watch television, while I thought television was a waste of time. Why not read a book and learn something? "What has anyone ever learned from watching television?" That was my perspective. She argued that watching television was her way of relaxing and, contrary to my opinion, there was a great deal one could learn from watching television. So, this became a "sore spot" in our relationship that periodically erupted into a full-blown argument. Through the years, we discovered many more sore spots. And our marriage became an ongoing series of verbal explosions.

In those days, I embraced the thought, "I have married the wrong person. Surely if I had married the right person, it would not be like this." I'm sure that Karolyn had the same thoughts. In talking with older couples, we later discovered that all marriages have conflicts. Some couples learn how to resolve conflicts in a friendly manner while others resort to heated arguments. We definitely fell into the last category.

For the past thirty-plus years, I have been sitting in my counseling office listening to other couples share their frustration with a lifestyle of arguments similar to what Karolyn and I experienced. Fortunately, I've been able to help many of them discover a better way. In this chapter, I will share some of the insights that I have shared with them.

First, we must begin by accepting the reality that we will have conflicts. Conflicts are not a sign that you have married the wrong person. They simply affirm that you are human. We all tend to assume that our ideas are the best ideas. What we fail to recognize is that our spouse has the same opinion of their ideas. Their logic will not agree with your logic, and their emotions will not mirror your own. Our ideas and perceptions of life are influenced by our history, our values, and our personality. And these factors are different for each of us.

Some of our conflicts will be major; some of our conflicts will be minor. The conflict over how to load a dishwasher falls into the minor category. The conflict over whether or not to have a baby is definitely in the major league. Large or small, all conflicts have the potential of destroying an evening, a week, a month, or a lifetime. On the other hand, conflicts have the potential of teaching us how to love, support, and encourage each other. This is by far the better road to travel. The difference is in how you process the conflicts.

Once you have accepted the reality of conflicts, you need to discover a healthy plan for processing your conflicts. Such a plan begins with recognizing the need to listen. When most of us have conflicts, we feel the need to talk, but talking without listening leads to arguments. The real need is the need to listen. I remember the wife who said to me, "The most helpful thing that came out of our first counseling session with you was the idea of requesting a 'listening time.' Before that I had always said to my husband, 'We need to talk.' That sentence always put him in a bad mood. Now I say, 'At your convenience, I would like to request a time that I can listen to you.' He never waits long until he says to me, 'So, you want to listen to my ideas, right?' 'Yes,' I respond and we set a time for listening. Requesting a time for listening creates a much different atmosphere."

"So, how does your listening time begin?" I asked. "He normally says, 'So, you want to listen? What's the topic?' Then I say, 'The topic is, how are we going to spend the Christmas holidays?', or whatever conflict I have on my mind. We have agreed to discuss only one topic at a time. He shares what he wants to do during the holidays, and I genuinely try to understand not only what he is suggesting but why he is suggesting it and how important it is to him. I often ask questions to clarify his statements such as, 'Are you saying that you want us to spend Christmas with your parents because your father has cancer and you don't anticipate he will be here next Christmas?' Once I've asked all my questions to clarify what he is saying, I then respond, 'That makes a lot of sense. I can understand that.'

"Then he says, 'Now that you know what's on my mind, I would like to have a listening time to hear your perspective on the topic.' So I share my perspective while he listens and tries to understand. He may also ask questions to clarify such as, 'Are you saying that you want us to spend Christmas with your parents because your sister from California is going to be there and she only comes once every five years and you would hate to miss this opportunity to spend time with her?' Once he's asked all his questions and listens to my responses, he says to me, 'That makes a lot of sense. I think I understand what you're saying.' We have not yet resolved our differences, but we do understand each other and have affirmed each other's ideas. We are no longer enemies. We have refused to argue. We are friends who are now going to look for a solution to our conflict."

What this wife described to me was the process that I have

taught many couples in my counseling office through the years. It is based on the concept of showing genuine respect for the other individual, giving them full freedom to think their own thoughts, have their own opinions, and have their own reasons for these opinions. It is expressing understanding and affirming that their ideas make sense. It takes away the adversarial atmosphere in resolving conflicts and creates an atmosphere of friendship.

In marriage it is never "having my way." It is rather discovering "our" way.

After you have heard and affirmed each other's ideas, you are now ready to look for a solution to the conflict. The big word in finding a solution is "compromise." Often we think of the word compromise as a negative word. People are often warned about compromising their values or beliefs. However, compromise in a marriage is not only positive but it is necessary. Compromise means to find a meeting place. It requires each of you to be willing to give up something in order to have harmony in the marriage. If, on the other hand, we both insist on having our way, then we are back in the argument mode. In marriage it is never "having my way." It is rather discovering "our" way.

"Meeting in the Middle"

In the illustration above, the couple agreed that if they flew instead of driving, they could spend three days at each of their parents' during the Christmas holidays. However, this meant they had to come up with the money for the airline tickets, which was not in their budget. After sharing several ideas, they finally agreed to change their summer vacation plans for a trip to the Caribbean and take a less expensive vacation in the state where they lived. Then they could use the money they would have used on their vacation to purchase the tickets for the Christmas holidays. They reasoned, "We can go to the Caribbean another year, but this year it seems really important that we both be with our families over Christmas." They both were willing to sacrifice their plans in order to do something that would be harmonious over the Christmas holidays. There is always a solution to conflicts. Two individuals who choose to be friends will find that solution.

Typically, there are three ways to resolve conflicts, once you are seeking them. One we have just described. You find a meeting place by agreeing to do a part of what each of you desired while each of you also sacrifices a bit. In the illustration above, they each sacrificed the idea of spending the entire holiday with one set of parents. And yet, they both received part of what they desired—contact with their parents and extended family over the holidays. Often conflicts are resolved in this manner. I call this approach "meeting in the middle." It involves finding a meeting place in the middle of your original ideas that both of you agree is workable.

"Meeting on Your Side"

A second way to resolve conflicts is what I call "meeting on your side." This means that after you hear each other's ideas and feelings, one of you decides that on this occasion, it is best to do what the other has in mind. This is a total sacrifice of your original idea, choosing rather to do what your spouse desires and to do it with a positive attitude. You are choosing to do what they desire as an act of love because you care about them and you see how important it is to them. One husband said, "I agreed to have a baby after she explained to me that she was getting near the end of her fertility cycle. When I saw her heart, I didn't want to take the chance of disappointing her. We had always agreed that we wanted to have children. I just thought it wasn't the right time. I wanted to wait until we had a better financial base. But as I listened to her and saw how important it was to her, I agreed that even though I had some fears, I thought we should go ahead and try to have a baby now. We did and I have never regretted that decision." Sometimes the decision to agree with the other person's idea will involve great sacrifice. However, love always involves some sacrifice.

"Can we just agree that for the moment, we disagree on this?"

"Meeting Later"

A third way of resolving a conflict is what I call "meeting later." This approach says, "At the moment, I'm not able to conscientiously agree with your idea, and I don't see a place to meet in the middle. Can we just agree that for the moment, we disagree on this? And we will discuss it again in a week or month, and look for a solution. In the meantime, we will love each other, enjoy each other, and support each other. This will not be a disruptive factor in our marriage." This is a perfectly legitimate response to a conflict when, at the moment, you cannot find a long-term solution. A month from now, things may look different or new possibilities may come to mind so that you can find a compromise with which both of you will feel good.

In some areas of life, "meeting later" can be a permanent solution, especially in areas where there is no "right" or "wrong" answer, whether it is squeezing the toothpaste tube, loading the dishwasher, or personal tastes in entertainment. Essentially, we agree to disagree on what is the logical thing to do, and we choose a practical solution. So that, for instance, you can agree that when he loads it, he can load it his way; when she loads it, she can load it her way. Or one night let her pick the movie and on another night let him do the selecting.

In one of these three ways, you can resolve your conflicts. The key, of course, is creating a friendly atmosphere by listening to each other and affirming each other's perspective rather than accusing each other of illogical thinking. When we learn to affirm each other's ideas and look for solutions, we can process the normal conflicts in a marriage relationship and learn to work together as a team. I wish someone had told me how to do this before Karolyn and I got married. It would have saved hours of wasted and meaningless arguments.

Talking It Over

1. Have you encountered any conflicts in your relationship in the past few months?
2. How did you resolve them?
3. At this point in your relationship, do you have any unresolved conflicts?
4. Memorize this question and use it the next time you have a conflict: "How can we resolve this conflict so that both of us feel loved and appreciated?"
5. In this chapter, we discussed three positive ways to resolve conflicts:
   - "Meeting in the middle"
   - "Meeting on your side"
   - "Meeting later"

Did you use any of these strategies in resolving a recent conflict? Did each of you feel loved and appreciated?

6. Can you think of an illustration where "meeting later" or "agreeing to disagree" might become a solution to one of your conflicts?

7. In your opinion, how well are the two of you doing in reaching win-win solutions when you have disagreements? What do you need to change or continue in order to improve?

5

I Wish I Had Known . . .

That APOLOGIZING *is a sign of* STRENGTH

My father was a fan of John Wayne. He saw one of Wayne's last movies, *True Grit*, where Wayne proclaimed, "Real men don't apologize." My dad took John Wayne to be a true prophet and followed his example. My father was a good man. He was not an abuser. He was not even an angry man. But from time to time, he would lose his temper and speak harshly to my mother and sometimes to my sister and me. In his eighty-six years, I never remember hearing him apologize. So I simply followed his model, and John Wayne had another convert.

I don't mean that I made a conscious decision never to apologize. The fact is, the thought of apologizing never crossed my mind. Before marriage, I could not imagine ever doing or saying anything to my wife that would warrant an apology. After all,

I loved her. I intended to make her supremely happy and I was certain she would do the same for me. However, after marriage I discovered a part of me that I never knew existed. I found out that the woman whom I had married had ideas, some of which I considered to be stupid. And I told her so. I remember saying with a loud, harsh voice, "Karolyn, think. This is simply not logical." My words would spark a sharp response and we would be on a downward spiral.

I was simply doing what my father had done. I never apologized.

After such episodes, we would both go silent and not speak to each other for hours or sometimes days. After the passing of time, I would break the silence and begin to talk to her as though nothing had happened. We would have a few good days or months before there were more harsh words. I did not recognize it at the time but now I see clearly. I was simply doing what my father had done. I never apologized. In my mind, I blamed her for our altercations. Needless to say, in the early years, we did not have a good marriage.

Shortly after our wedding, I enrolled in seminary and began theological studies. It was in this context that I discovered that the Christian scriptures have a great deal to say about confession and repentance. *Confession* means to admit that what I did or failed to do is wrong. *Repentance* means that I consciously turn from that wrong and seek to do what is right. I was attracted by the boldness of John the apostle who said, "If we claim to be without sin, we deceive ourselves and the truth is not in us. If we confess our sins, [God] is faithful and just and will forgive us our sins and purify us from all unrighteousness."[1] I realized that I had allowed myself to be deceived. Blaming Karolyn for my outburst was evidence of my deception. I found great personal solace in confessing my sins to God. To be totally honest, it was much more difficult to learn to confess my failures to Karolyn.

However, over the next few months, I did learn to apologize and found that Karolyn was fully willing to forgive. In time, she too learned to apologize and I extended forgiveness. After spending a lifetime counseling other couples, I am convinced that there are no healthy marriages without apology and forgiveness. I draw this conclusion from the reality that all of us are human and humans sometimes do and say things that are demeaning to other people. These unloving words and actions create emotional barriers between the people involved. Those barriers do not go away with the passing of time. They are removed only when we apologize and the offended party chooses to forgive.

A few years ago I teamed up with another counselor, Dr. Jennifer Thomas, and did extensive research on the art of apologizing. We asked hundreds of people two questions. First, "When you apologize, what do you typically say or do?" Second, "When someone apologizes to you, what do you expect to hear them say or do?" Their answers fell into five categories. We call them "the five languages of apology." The evidence was clear—what one person considers to be an apology is not what another person considers to be an apology. Thus, couples often miss each other in their efforts to apologize. He says, "I'm sorry." She is thinking, "You certainly are. Now, is there anything else you would like to say?" She is waiting for an apology; he thinks he has already apologized.

All of us are human and humans sometimes do and say things that are demeaning to other people.

Typically, we learn our apology language from our parents. Little Cole pushes his sister Julia down the stairs. His mother says, "Cole, don't push your sister. Go tell her you are sorry." So little Cole says to Julia, "I'm sorry." When Cole is thirty-two and offends his wife, he is likely to say, "I'm sorry." He is doing what his mother taught him to do and he doesn't understand why his wife does not freely forgive him. However, his wife had a different mother. Her mother taught her to say, "I was wrong. Will you please forgive me?" This is what she is waiting for Cole to say. In her mind "I'm sorry" does not qualify as an apology.

Couples often miss each other in their efforts to apologize.

The Apology Languages

Here is a brief summary of the five apology languages that we discovered in our research.

1. *Expressing regret*

"I'm sorry" may well be the first words in expressing this apology language. However, you need to tell what you are sorry for. The words "I'm sorry," spoken alone, are much too general. For example, you might say, "I'm sorry that I came home an hour late. I know you have been waiting for me so we could go to the movie. I realize that we've already missed the first thirty minutes and you probably don't want to go now. I feel bad that I did not pay more attention to the time. I got busy with work at the office. I can't blame anyone but myself. I feel like I have let you down big time."

If you have lost your temper and spoken harshly, you might say, "I am sorry that I lost my temper and raised my voice. I know I came across very harsh and that I hurt you deeply. A husband should never talk that way to his wife. I feel like I have demeaned you. I can only imagine how hurt I would feel if you spoke to me in that way. You must be hurting deeply and I am so sorry that I hurt you."

This apology language is an emotional language. It is seeking to express to the other person your emotional pain that your words or behavior have hurt them deeply. If this is the apology language of the person you have offended, what they want to know is, "Do you understand how deeply your behavior has hurt me?" Anything short of this kind of apology will seem empty to them.

2. *Accepting Responsibility*

This apology begins with the words "I was wrong," and then goes on to explain what was wrong about your behavior. For example, "I was wrong not to plan my afternoon so I could get home early. I knew we were going out tonight but I didn't consciously think about what time I needed to be home in order for us to leave on time. It was my fault and it was wrong. I can't blame anyone else."

The person who has spoken harshly might apologize in the following manner. "The way I talked to you was wrong. It is not loving or kind to raise my voice and speak harshly to you. I should not have allowed my temper to get out of control. I'm not blaming you. I'm accepting responsibility for my behavior and I know it was wrong."

The person whose primary apology language is "accepting responsibility" is waiting to hear you admit your behavior was wrong. For this person, saying "I'm sorry" will never sound like an apology. They want you to be willing to accept responsibility for what you did or said and acknowledge that it was wrong.

3. *Making restitution*

This apology language seeks to "make it right." One husband who forgot their wedding anniversary said, "I know that I've really blown it. I can't believe that I actually forgot our anniversary. What kind of husband is that? I know that I can't undo what I have done but I would like an opportunity to make it up to you. I want you to think about it and let me know what I could do to make things right with you. We can go anywhere or do anything. You deserve the best and I want to give it to you." If "making restitution" is his wife's primary apology language, you can bet she will have an idea of what he can do to make things right.

For the person whose primary apology language is "making restitution," what they really want to know is "Do you still love me?" Your behavior seems so unloving to them that they wonder how you could love them and do what you did. Thus, what they request of you may well be in keeping with their love language. If their primary love language is *physical touch,* they may simply say to you "Would you just hold me or could we make love?" If, on the other hand, *receiving gifts* is their love language, they will likely request a gift that they had wanted, which to them would genuinely express your love. If *acts of service* is their love language, they may say "The greatest thing you could do to make it right with me is to clean out the garage." If *quality time* is their primary love language, they may well request a weekend away—just the two of you. The person for whom *words of affirmation* is their love language will ask you to verbally affirm your love. They may say "Could you just write me a love letter and tell me why you love me and how much you love me?" To them, words speak louder than actions.

4. *Genuinely expressing the desire to change your behavior*

This apology seeks to come up with a plan to keep the bad behavior from reoccurring. One man who "lost his temper again" said, "I don't like this about me. This is not good. I know I did the same thing last week. This has got to stop. You deserve better than this. Can you help me think what I can do to make sure that this doesn't happen again?" His desire for change communicates to his wife that he is sincerely apologizing.

This couple decided that when he felt himself getting "hot," he would say to her, "Honey, I've got to take a walk. I'll be back shortly." He would take the walk and calm down. When he came back in thirty minutes, he would say to her, "I love you so much and I appreciate the time out. I don't ever want to lose my temper with you again. I appreciate you helping me overcome this." In some people's eyes, if your apology does not include a desire to change your behavior, you have not truly apologized. Whatever else you say, they do not see it as being sincere. In their minds, if you are really apologizing, you will seek to change your behavior.

5. *Requesting forgiveness*

"Will you please forgive me?" These words are music to the ears of the person whose primary apology language is "requesting forgiveness." In their mind, if you are sincere, you will ask them to forgive you. This is what an apology is all about. You have hurt them and they want to know, "Do you want to be forgiven? Do you want to remove the barrier that your behavior has caused?" Requesting forgiveness is what touches their heart and rings of sincerity.

What Dr. Thomas and I discovered is that when couples learn how to apologize in a manner that is meaningful to the other person, they make forgiveness much easier. What most people want to know when you are attempting to apologize is "Are you sincere?" However, they judge your sincerity by whether or not you are speaking what to them is a genuine apology. That means you must learn to speak your apology in their primary apology language. When you do, they sense your real sincerity.

Carl Learns "I'm Sorry"

Learning to apologize effectively may not be easy. Some of you may identify with the following story taken from our book *The Five Languages of Apology*.

Carl, thinking about marriage, came to one of our seminars with his girlfriend, Melinda. After they completed apology questionnaires, Melinda told him that the thing she wants to hear most in an apology is "I'm sorry."

Later during the seminar, Carl approached me. "To be honest with you, I don't know if I've ever said those words. They sound kinda 'girly' to me. I've always been taught that real men don't apologize. I guess it is a macho thing.

"I'm not sure I can say those words, and Melinda seems to be concerned about it. Maybe we shouldn't have taken your apology questionnaire!" he joked.

"On the other hand, maybe it's really good that you did," I said with a chuckle. "Let me ask you a question. Have you ever done anything in your whole life that you really regretted? After doing this, did you say to yourself, 'I wish I hadn't done that'?"

He nodded and said, "Yes. I got drunk the night before my mother's funeral. So the next morning, I was suffering with a big hangover. I don't remember much about the funeral."

"How did you feel about that?" I asked.

"Really bad," Carl said. "I really felt like I dishonored my mother. Her death hit me very hard. We had always been close and I could talk with her about things. I guess I was just trying to drown my sorrow, but I had too much to drink. I know that would have made her sad. She always talked to me about drinking too much. I was hoping that people in heaven didn't know what was going on here on earth, because I didn't want to hurt her."

I was hoping that people in heaven didn't know what was going on here on earth, because I didn't want to hurt her.

"Suppose for a moment that people in heaven do know what's happening on earth, that your mother really was disappointed in your behavior and what you did. And let's suppose that you had a chance to talk with her. What would you say?"

Carl's eyes moistened, and he said, "I'd tell her that I'm really sorry that I let her down. I know that was not a time for drinking. I wish I could go back and relive that night. I wouldn't have gone to the bar. I'd tell her that I really love her and I hope that she would forgive me."

I put my arm on Carl's shoulder, and I said, "Do you know what you just did?"

He started nodding his head and said, "Yeah. I just apologized to my mother. It feels good. Do you think she heard me?" he asked.

"I think she did," I said, "and I think she's forgiven you."

"Doggone. I didn't mean to cry," he said, wiping tears from his cheeks.

"That's another thing; you were taught that real men don't cry, right?"

"Yeah."

"You've gotten some bad information through the years, Carl," I said. "Fact is, real men do cry. It's plastic men who don't cry. Real men do apologize. They even say 'I'm sorry' when they realize they've hurt someone they love. You are a real man, Carl. You've demonstrated it today. Don't ever forget it. If you and Melinda get married, you won't be a perfect husband and she won't be a perfect wife. It's not necessary to be perfect in order to have a good marriage. But it is necessary to apologize when you do things that hurt each other. And if saying 'I'm sorry' is Melinda's primary apology language, then you will need to learn to speak it."

"Got it!" he said with a smile. "I'm glad we came to this seminar."

"So am I," I said as he walked away.

One year later, I was leading a seminar in Columbia, South Carolina. Early on Saturday morning before anyone else had arrived, in walked Carl and Melinda. "We came early hoping we would have a chance to talk with you," he said. "We just want to tell you how much your seminar meant to us last year when you were in Summerfield. It was a big changing point in our relationship. We got married three months after the seminar, and the things we learned that day keep coming back to us."

"I'm not sure we would still be married if we had not attended the seminar," Melinda said. "I had no idea the first year of marriage would be so hard."

"Tell me," I said, "does Carl know how to apologize?"

"Oh, yes. We're both good apologizers," she said. "That's one of the main things we learned that day—that and the five love languages. Those two things have helped us survive."

Carl said, "It wasn't easy for me. But the day I apologized to my mother was a big breakthrough for me. I realized how important it was to be honest about my behavior."

"What is your love language?" I asked Melinda.

"Acts of service," she said, "and Carl is getting really good at it. He even washes and folds the towels."

"Both of us want to grow old together. That's why we're back today for a refresher class."

Carl shook his head and said, "I never thought I'd be doing that. But I'll have to admit, doing laundry is a whole lot easier than saying, 'I'm sorry.' But I've learned to do both of them. I want us to have a good marriage. My folks never had a good marriage, nor did Melinda's. Both of us want to grow old together. That's why we're back today for a refresher class. We're looking forward to learning some new things."

"You are a real man," I said as I patted him on the back.[2]

Looking back on my own marriage, I wish I had known not only the importance of apology, but how to apologize effectively. It would have saved me many days of silent suffering, hoping in vain that Karolyn would forget my harsh words.

Talking It Over

1. Do you remember the last time you apologized? If so, what did you say?

2. Do you remember the last time someone apologized to you? Did it seem sincere? Did you forgive the person? Why or why not?

3. Discuss with each other what you expect to hear in a sincere apology.
4. Presently, is there anything for which you need to apologize? Why not do it today?

I Wish I Had Known . . .

That FORGIVENESS *is not a* FEELING

The only healthy response to an apology is forgiveness. But what does it mean to forgive? Before I got married, I thought that forgiveness was letting go of the hurt and, thus, restoring the feelings of love. It seemed rather easy to me. I remember once when Karolyn called and broke a date with me saying that she needed to go shopping with a girlfriend, I was crushed and angry. How could she think that a shopping trip with a girlfriend was more important than our spending the evening together?

I lived with the pain of hurt and anger for two days until we had our next date. The evening had not progressed very far when she asked, “Is something wrong?” I opened the floodgates of my emotions and “let it all hang out.” I told her how disappointed I was that she would choose a shopping trip with a friend over our time together.

When I finished my display of emotion, she said to me in the kindest way, "I'm sorry. I should have explained it more fully to you. It wasn't that I didn't want to be with you. That was the only weekend my girlfriend had off from work and she needed my help in purchasing a birthday gift for her mother. I knew that you and I could get together another night. I didn't mean to hurt you. I'd rather be with you any night than go shopping. I hope you will forgive me." Like a paper towel soaking up water, her speech and apology evaporated all of my hurt. And I was overcome with warm feelings of love. It was over. Our relationship was restored and I never thought of it again. In my mind, that's what it meant to forgive.

However, after we were married forgiveness seemed much more difficult. One evening about six weeks after our wedding, Karolyn and I were engaged in a full-fledged argument. In the midst of the argument, she went to a closet, got her raincoat, slammed the front door, and walked out into the pouring rain. My first thought was, "Why doesn't she stay and fight like a man?" But my second thought was, "Oh, no. What if she doesn't come back?" My tears flowed freely as I wondered, "How could it have come to this so early in our marriage?" I flipped on the TV and tried to forget the ordeal, but there was no forgetting.

After what seemed like an eternity, I heard the door open and I turned to see her crying. "I'm sorry I walked out on you but I just couldn't take it any longer. I hate arguing. When you yelled at me, I knew I had to get out or it would get worse." I apologized to her for raising my voice but in my heart, I blamed her for the whole argument. We went to bed with our backs toward each other.

The next day after time to reflect, I apologized more fully to her and she apologized to me. We both said, "I forgive you." But the hurt did not evaporate, and the warm feelings of love did not return. For the next few weeks, I relived the episode. I could not get out of my mind the picture of her walking into the rain nor could I remove the sound of the slamming of the door. Each time I replayed the scene, the hurt returned.

As a recent college graduate, I had never taken a course on the topic of forgiveness. Nor did I remember ever seeing a book on the topic. I simply knew that our statements of forgiveness to each other had not restored the feeling of love. Now, after more than thirty years as a marriage counselor, I have learned a great deal about forgiveness. In this chapter I want to share those insights. Let's start at the beginning.

What Forgiveness Is—and Isn't

Forgiveness presupposes that a wrong has been committed. Irritations do not call for forgiveness; rather, they call for negotiation. However, when one of you speaks or behaves unkindly to the other, it calls for an apology and forgiveness if the relationship is to be restored. There are minor offenses and major offenses but the process is always the same. When one of us offends the other, an emotional barrier is erected between the two of us.

> In the Jewish and Christian scriptures, there are three Hebrew words and four Greek words that are translated as *forgive*.

The passing of time will never remove the barrier. Barriers are removed by sincere apologies and genuine forgiveness. In the last chapter we talked about how to apologize sincerely. In this chapter, we are talking about what it means to forgive.

In the Jewish and Christian scriptures, there are three Hebrew words and four Greek words that are translated as *forgive.* They are synonyms with various shades of meaning. The most basic idea is "to pardon," or "to take away." When speaking of God forgiving us, the scriptures say, "As far as the east is from the west, so far has [God] removed our transgressions from us."[1] Forgiveness removes the barrier, and lifts the penalty. No longer does God demand that we pay for our wrongdoing. When we sincerely apologize and request His forgiveness, He pardons us and will never again hold that failure against us.

Forgiveness does not destroy our memory.

We are instructed to forgive each other in the same way that God forgives us. Thus, forgiveness is not a feeling but a decision. It is the decision to offer grace instead of demanding justice. Forgiveness removes the barrier and opens the possibility for the relationship to grow.

Perhaps I could better explain forgiveness by sharing four things that forgiveness does not do.

First, *forgiveness does not destroy our memory.* I have sometimes heard people say, "If you have not forgotten, you have not forgiven." That statement is untrue. The human brain records every experience, good and bad, pleasant and unpleasant. Psychologists have explained the human mind as having two compartments. One is called the conscious mind, and the other, the subconscious mind. The conscious mind is composed of those things that you are conscious of in this moment. For example, I am fully aware that at the moment I am sitting in a chair. If I choose, I could share with you the sights and sounds that are around me. The subconscious mind houses past experiences that are stored in mental files.

Some data flows freely from the subconscious to the conscious mind. At a given time, we may choose to bring data from the subconscious to the conscious. For example, if you ask me "What did you eat for breakfast?" I could reach into the subconscious mind and tell you "I had Cheerios with blueberries." Before you asked the question, I was not consciously thinking of breakfast. But at will, I could retrieve that information.

Other experiences are buried deep in the subconscious and may be difficult to retrieve even with effort. On the other hand, sometimes memories leap from the subconscious to the conscious mind without being requested. This is often true of hurtful memories. Even after you have chosen to pardon their behavior and remove the barrier, the memory of the event may leap back into your conscious mind, and with the memory comes the feeling of hurt and perhaps anger. The memory does not mean that you have not forgiven. It means simply that you are human and remembering a painful experience.

How do we handle these painful memories? My suggestion is that you take them to God and say, "Father, You know what I am remembering and You know the feelings that I have. But I thank You that all of that has been forgiven. Now help me to do something today that will enhance our relationship." In this prayer, you are affirming the decision to forgive and you are seeking to foster growth in the future.

Second, *forgiveness does not remove all the consequences of wrongdoing*. For example, a mother has saved money for surgery. Her son steals it and spends it on drugs. If he sincerely apologizes, she can forgive him—but the money is still gone. A father abandons his wife and children. Twenty years later, he comes back to apologize. They can forgive him—but it does not restore the twenty lost years. The husband in anger physically abuses his wife, breaking her jaw. He may sincerely apologize and she may forgive him—but her jaw is still broken.

Forgiveness does not remove all the consequences of wrong behavior.

All of our behavior has consequences. Positive behavior has positive consequences. Negative behavior has negative consequences. Forgiveness does not remove all the consequences of wrong behavior.

Third, *forgiveness does not rebuild trust.* A husband who had been sexually unfaithful to his wife later broke off the affair and apologized to his wife. She said to me in the counseling office, "I think I have forgiven him, but I don't trust him. That makes me wonder if I have really forgiven him." The fact is, forgiveness does not automatically restore trust. Trust is that gut-level confidence that someone is a person of integrity. Trust in a relationship is destroyed when one partner is unfaithful. When you do not keep your commitments to me, I lose trust in you. I no longer have the confidence that you will treat me fairly and honestly. How then is trust rebuilt? By changing your behavior and by being trustworthy. Over a period of time, if I see you are doing what you say you will do and being open and aboveboard in all of our dealings, I come again to trust you.

When I am counseling a couple in which one of them has been sexually unfaithful and is now seeking to rebuild a marriage, I recommend, after a sincere apology and forgiveness, that the offending party give the spouse permission to examine every area of life. That means that the checkbook, the computer, the iPhone, and all other sources of information are available for the spouse's examination. With this action you are saying, "I have nothing to hide; I have truly changed my behavior, and I want to be worthy of your trust again." With this attitude of openness and a consistent pattern of honesty, trust can be restored. Thus, forgiveness does not automatically restore trust, but forgiveness does open the door to the possibility that trust can be regained.

Fourth, *forgiveness does not always result in reconciliation.* The word reconciliation means "to bring back to harmony." Reconciliation requires working through differences, finding new ways of doing things, solving the conflicts of the past, and learning how to work together as a team. How long does it take to be reconciled? That depends largely on how long the two of you have been "out of harmony." For some, it may only take hours; for others, it may take months. For some, it will require the help of a professional counselor because the two of them do not have the skills to rebuild their relationship. What I am saying is that forgiveness does not automatically bring harmony in the relationship. However, it does open the possibility of reconciliation.

I began this chapter by saying that forgiveness is the only healthy response to an apology. If we choose not to forgive, then the barrier remains and the relationship is estranged. Time alone will not heal the relationship. Healing requires the decision to forgive. And forgiveness opens the door to the possibility of growth.

What if the person who has offended you does not apologize?

I want to conclude this chapter by asking one other question. What if the person who has offended you does not apologize? The most positive approach you can take is to lovingly confront them with their offense and hope that they will apologize and you can forgive. If your first attempt fails, I suggest you make a second and third attempt. An apology says, "I value this relationship, and I want to deal with this problem." The refusal to apologize says, "I do not value this relationship, and it's okay with me if we continue to be estranged." We cannot force an apology but we can extend the olive branch and express our willingness to forgive. If, in the final analysis, they are unwilling to restore the relationship, you may then release them to God and release your hurt and anger to Him. Don't allow their unwillingness to deal with the problem destroy your life. It takes two people to build a positive, healthy relationship.

Had I known what I've shared with you in this chapter before I got married, I would have been a much better forgiver. I would have understood and processed my emotions in a healthier manner. I would have understood that forgiveness does not remove all the hurt nor does it automatically restore loving feelings. But forgiveness is the first step in processing hurt and restoring love. There are no healthy marriages without sincere apologies and genuine forgiveness. If you learn how to apologize and forgive, you will have in place two of the major elements for building a successful marriage.

Talking It Over

1. Is there someone you need to lovingly confront? What keeps you from doing so?
2. Is there someone you have not yet forgiven? What keeps you from doing so?
3. What barriers stand between you and someone you love? What will you do to remove the barriers?
4. When someone apologizes to you, how easy is it for you to forgive? Why?

7

I Wish I Had Known . . .

That TOILETS *are not* SELF-CLEANING

In the home in which I grew up, the toilet was never dirty. It never crossed my mind that someone was cleaning it. To this day, I don't know whether it was my mother or my father. I never saw anyone cleaning the toilet. Two weeks after Karolyn and I got married, I enrolled in graduate school and we lived in student housing. It was a small apartment but it was clean and nice. About three weeks later, I noticed that the toilet had dark stains. (By this time I knew that toilets had to be cleaned. After all, I was in graduate school.) I mentioned it to Karolyn and she said, "I know. I was wondering when you were going to clean it." "Clean it?!" I said. "I thought you were going to clean it. I don't know how to clean a toilet." "Well then, let me teach you," she said. "Can't we get something that will automatically clean it when it flushes?" I asked. "Those things don't work," she answered. "They're a waste of money."

Before marriage, I never considered the idea that I would someday be a toilet cleaner. Actually, I became so good at it that the second semester, I got a part-time job with a professional toilet cleaning company. And I went from business to business, cleaning toilets. After I got professional training, cleaning our little toilet in our little apartment was a breeze.

Confusion over roles is one of the most stressful aspects of contemporary marriages.

Let me ask you a personal question. If and when you get married, who do you think will clean the toilet in your apartment or house? I have discovered in premarital counseling that most men think the wife will clean it, while most women think their husband will clean it. Without premarital counseling, most couples never even think about who will clean the toilet and three weeks after the wedding, they too discover that toilets are not self-cleaning.

Who Does What?

I raise this issue not because I am overly concerned about who will clean the toilet. However, I am greatly concerned that you will enter marriage never having discussed *who* is going to do *what* after you get married. It is what the sociologists call "marital roles." Confusion over roles is one of the most stressful aspects of contemporary marriages. In earlier generations where the husband was the provider and the wife the homemaker, there was little confusion about who would do what. However, in today's world, where most young wives have their own careers, they expect their husbands to be majorly involved in household duties. If the two of you do not discuss and agree upon who will do what, you will find this to be a major source of conflict in the early months of marriage.

There are several factors that come into play when you discuss marital roles. First, the two of you grew up with different models. One young wife said, "My father always vacuumed the floors every Saturday morning before he washed the car. Now, my husband expects me to vacuum the floors, and he wants me to run the car through the automatic car wash. I can't believe I married such a lazy man." Her husband said, "My mother vacuumed the floors. It never crossed my mind that my wife would ever expect me to do that. And as for the car, it's a matter of efficiency. Why should I spend two hours washing the car every Saturday when I can run it through a car wash in three minutes for $3? In my family, we never washed a car. Every three months, we would pay $12 and get a thorough washing. I don't know why this is such a big deal to her."

It was a big deal for her because, in her mind, he was not being a responsible husband. Her expectations made no sense to him because in the family in which he grew up, he had a different model. One of the learning exercises that I have done in premarital counseling is to have the woman make a list of all the things her father did around the house and all the responsibilities that her mother accepted. I asked the young man to do the same. Once the lists are made, we examine them to see where their parental models are similar and different. Then I challenge the couple to have a lengthy discussion on how they expect their own marriage to be similar and different from their parental models. To ignore or to deny the influence of parental models on your own expectations is a sign of immaturity. The mature couple will openly and honestly share their own expectations and, where they have differences of opinion, will negotiate an agreement about marital roles before they get married.

Where Do These Ideas Come From?

A second influence upon your perception of marital roles is your own philosophy about maleness and femaleness. Your philosophy answers the question, "What does a man do and what does a woman do in a marriage relationship?" Your answer to this question has been greatly influenced by your educational experience. For example, if she attended a university where she was exposed to strong feminist professors, then she will likely have very strong opinions about what women do and don't do in a marriage relationship. On the other hand, if she attended a conservative religious university, she will likely have very different ideas as to the role of a woman in marriage. His education and religious beliefs will also greatly influence his philosophy of the role of the man and the woman in a marriage. To ignore these strongly held philosophies or to think that your love will override their influence is foolish. If you cannot negotiate these differences before marriage, they will greatly inhibit your ability to develop marital unity.

If he feels embarrassed to let his friends know that he washes dishes and she feels that washing dishes is a sign of masculinity, then washing dishes will become an emotional stress on their relationship. If she feels strongly that a wife should not do all the cooking and he, on the other hand, has no expertise in cooking, they need to negotiate an agreement before marriage. Either she changes her opinion or he enrolls in a culinary course at the local community college. Your philosophy of maleness and femaleness greatly influences your expectations of marital roles.

What Are Each of You Good At?

This brings me to the third factor that will influence your opinion on who should do what, and that is the reality that both of you have different skills. When it comes to food preparation, one of you may be skilled at shopping for the best deals while the other may simply buy whatever is necessary to prepare the meal. One of you may be skilled at baking while the other is skilled at grilling. One knows how to dust furniture and the other can't see dust. One of you may know how to trim shrubbery and landscape the yard and the other may not have a clue. One is a computer whiz and the other simply knows how to send emails.

It is important to recognize these differing abilities and seek to use them for the benefit of the relationship.

We need not have the same skill sets, but it is important to recognize these differing abilities and seek to use them for the benefit of the relationship. On a football team, all eleven players have the same objective, but they don't all play the same role. The coach seeks to put the players in the position that he thinks they are best equipped to execute. That principle should also be helpful in determining marital roles.

Likes—and Dislikes

The fourth factor in finding agreement about who will do what is the simple fact that each of you has likes and dislikes. She may find budgeting and keeping track of finances to be a breeze, where he may find it to be an ordeal. They both have the skills to add, subtract, and keep records, but one of them likes to do it and the other does not. He may find vacuuming the floors an invigorating challenge; she may find it drudgery. She may find paying the monthly bills to be enjoyable; he may find it as extremely oppressive. Making sure that we know each other's likes and dislikes is an important step in the process of deciding marital roles. Ideally, it would be nice to have each of you doing things that you enjoy doing. But if neither of you enjoys doing it, obviously someone must accept responsibility for a task that is not necessarily pleasant. However, considering each other's likes and dislikes should be a part of the process in deciding who will do what.

A Practical Exercise

Now I want to give you a practical exercise that will help you decide not only who will clean the toilet but who will do all the other things that are necessary. If you are seriously contemplating marriage, make a list of all the things that come to mind that will have to be done in order to maintain a household. Be sure to include your vehicles and who will purchase and prepare the food, do the laundry, and vacuum the floors. Ask your fiancé to make a similar list. Then bring the two lists together and make a master list that includes everything the two of you listed.

> If you can't agree before marriage, what makes you think you will agree after marriage?

Make two copies of this list and, individually and separately, sit down with the list and put your initials beside those items that you think will be your responsibility. If you think it will be a shared responsibility, put both of your initials but underline the one that you think will have the primary responsibility. Once you have completed this task, set aside an evening to work through your answers and see where you have agreed or disagreed on who will have the primary responsibility on each item. Where you have disagreements, it calls for negotiation. Share with each other your reasons for the choice you made. Be as open and honest as you can about what brought you to that conclusion. After listening to each other empathetically, then seek to make an agreement on who will accept that responsibility. (If you can't agree before marriage, what makes you think you will agree after marriage?)

Completing this assignment does not mean that you are locked into these responsibilities for the rest of your life. After six months of marriage, you may want to renegotiate some of these things. But it does mean you will enter marriage with a better understanding of your expectations of each other. Completing these exercises and reaching agreement on who will do what will save you many conflicts and make life flow much more harmoniously for both of you.

Talking It Over

1. If you grew up with your father, what responsibilities did he accept in the family?

2. What responsibilities did your mother accept?

3. If you are seriously considering marriage, complete the assignment described above.

8

I Wish I Had Known . . .

That we needed a **PLAN** *for* **HANDLING** *our* **MONEY**

When Karolyn and I were dating and later decided to get married, it never crossed my mind that we needed to discuss how we would handle our finances. Neither of us had any money. After all, we both were recent college graduates. During college we both lived in dormitories. I had never rented an apartment, never paid an electric bill, never had a car payment, and seldom ever bought clothes. I worked a part-time job to pay for my college expenses. After my junior year my parents were kind enough to buy me a car and pay the insurance. The clothes I wore came as gifts from my family at Christmas and on birthdays. Karolyn's experience was similar except that before enrolling in college, she worked full-time for one year, had her own apartment, and paid her own bills.

The only financial plan we had was that she had agreed to work full-time while I pursued graduate studies full-time. That plan lasted for two months. Karolyn's job required her to begin work at 5:30 a.m. She is not a "morning person." Her health was spiraling downward, and we both agreed that this plan was not working. We decided that we would both look for part-time, afternoon jobs. She rather quickly was hired by one of my professors at the university, and I found a job at the local bank. Neither of us made a lot of money, but it was enough to pay the rent on our student apartment, the utilities, and gas for the car, as well as put food on the table. Neither of us bought any clothes for three years. When I finished my graduate studies and began my first full-time employment, we had a grand total of $150.

In those years, we had no money problems because we had no money.

In those years, we had no money problems because we had no money. As long as a couple agrees to sacrifice temporarily in order to reach a stated objective, in our case graduate school, and as long as there is enough income to pay for the necessities, they are not likely to have marital struggles about money. Our struggles came after we started "making money."

We still had never discussed a plan for handling our money. After three years of sacrifice, we were both excited about spending. However, we had very different ideas about what purchases we should make and when. With no plan in place, finances became for us what it has become for many couples—a battlefield. I will not bore you with our specific skirmishes. The point I'm making is that if we had developed a plan before marriage, we would have saved ourselves a lot of useless fighting. The plan that

I will share in the rest of this chapter is a simple plan of money management that has helped thousands of couples avoid financial warfare. Let's start at the beginning.

"Our Money": Building Unity

The first foundational stone in developing a financial plan is to agree that after marriage, it will no longer be "my money" and "your money" but "our money." At the heart of marriage is the desire for unity. "For better or for worse," we intend to live life together. The implication is that we will share our income and work as a team in deciding what to do with our money. Incidentally, this also means that his and her debts will become "our debts," and we have the responsibility to develop a plan to repay these debts. It also implies that his and her savings will become "our savings." If you are not ready for this kind of unity, then you are not ready for marriage.

Saving, Sharing, Spending

The second step in developing a financial plan is to agree on a percentage of income that you will save, give away, and spend. There are essentially only three things you can do with money. You can save it, you can give it away, or you can spend it. Deciding the percentage that you will allocate to each of these categories is an important step in making a financial plan.

> His and her debts will become "our debts."

Through the years, I have encouraged couples to adopt the "10-10-80 Plan." Save and invest 10 percent of your net income. The first purpose of saving is to have emergency funds in case of sickness or loss of job. The second purpose of saving is to pay off any credit card and consumer debts that the two of you may have. The third purpose of saving is in order to make major purchases such as home and automobile. (Retirement saving is normally a part of one's employment package. I strongly encourage couples to participate in whatever retirement plan is offered by their employer.)

Another 10 percent is to be given away. The purpose of giving is to express gratitude for what has been given to you. The ancient Jewish and Christian traditions encourage the giving of 10 percent of one's income. The happiest people in the world are not those who have the most money but those who have learned the satisfaction of giving to help others. An early Christian text says, "It is more blessed to give than to receive."[1]

For Karolyn and me, the giving of 10 percent of our income was never a struggle. We had both been taught that principle by our parents and had practiced it as individuals. Thus, we freely agreed that this would be the pattern of our giving. Neither of us has ever regretted this decision. However, if this concept is new to one of you, it will take discussion and negotiation to find a meeting place on this concept. If you can't agree on 10 percent, then what percentage can you agree to give? The process of negotiation and agreement before marriage will save you from struggling with this issue after marriage.

> The most common mistake young couples make is to purchase a house that is beyond their income.

The Other 80 Percent

That leaves 80 percent to be divided among mortgage payments (or rent), utilities, insurance, furniture, food, clothes, transportation, medicine, recreation, etc. How this is distributed is your decision. The more you spend on housing, the less you have to spend in other areas. The most common mistake young couples make is to purchase a house that is beyond their income.

Before marriage, it is difficult to know the exact cost of housing and utilities and many of the other categories listed above. I have often encouraged couples who are contemplating marriage to find a couple who has been married about three years and is living in an apartment or house similar to what you would contemplate buying or renting. Let them share with you the approximate cost of housing and utilities. They may also be willing to give you a list of their other expenditures. This will give you a somewhat realistic idea of what to expect. A common guideline is to spend no more than 40 percent of your net income on housing and utilities.

Wise shopping does make a difference. In spite of the jokes we hear about the wife who spends $5 on gas driving to an outlet store where she saves $2, the wise shopper can realize substantial savings. Such shopping takes time and energy. It is work and involves a great deal of insight. But the benefit will be revealed in extra money that can be applied to other needs or wants. Mastering the art of good shopping is worth the effort involved. For practical help on how to shop wisely see *The Little Book of Big Savings.*[2]

Another extremely important matter that needs to be discussed by every couple is credit buying. If I had a red flag, I would wave it here. The media screams from every corner: "Buy now, pay later." What is not stated is that if you buy now without cash, you will pay much more later. Interest rates on charge accounts have a wide range. Many are in the 18–21 percent bracket. Couples need to read the small print. Credit is a privilege for which you must pay, and the cost is not the same on all plans.

One guiding principle is, if you have a credit card, use it only for emergencies (medical treatment) and necessities (car repairs, major appliances). Then, pay off the balance as quickly as possible. Never use the card for non-essentials—instead, save and pay cash. Some financial advisers suggest that couples never own a credit card. However, the all-important FICO score actually can score you lower if you have no credit history. This can be a problem when you get ready to purchase a house, car, or major appliance.

Why do we use credit? Because we want *now* what we cannot pay for now.

The credit card has been for many couples a membership card to "the society of the financially frustrated." It encourages impulse buying, and most of us have more impulses than we can afford to follow. I know that credit cards can aid in keeping records and that, if payments are made in full promptly, charges are minimal. Most couples, however, will spend more and stretch out payments longer if they regularly use credit cards.

Why do we use credit? Because we want *now* what we cannot pay for now. In the purchase of a house, that may be a wise financial move. We would have to pay rent anyway. If the house is well selected, it will appreciate in value. If we have money for the down payment and can afford the monthly payments, such a purchase is wise. On the other hand, most of our purchases do not appreciate in value. Their value begins to decrease the day we buy them. We buy them before we can afford them. We pay the purchase price, plus the interest charges for credit, while the article itself continues to depreciate in value.

I know that there are certain "necessities" in our society, but why should a young couple think they must obtain in the first year of their marriage what it took their parents thirty years to accumulate? Why must you have the biggest and the best now? With such a philosophy, you destroy the joy of aspiration and attainment. The necessities of life are relatively few. They can be met on your present income. (If you are unemployed, our society has help for you. The poorest in this country can have the necessities.) I am not opposed to aspiring for more and better "things" if these can be used for good. But I am suggesting that you live in the present rather than the future. Leave the future joys for future accomplishments. Enjoy today what you have today.

For many years my wife and I have played a little game that we have come to enjoy. It is called "Let's see how many things we can do without that everyone else thinks they must have." It all started in graduate school days out of necessity, but we got hooked and have continued to play it.

The game works like this. On Friday night or Saturday, you go together to the department store and walk down the aisles, looking at whatever catches your eye. Read the labels, talk about how fascinating each item is, and turn to each other and say, "Isn't it great that we don't have to have that?" Then while others walk out with arms loaded, names duly signed, you walk out hand in hand, excited that you do not need things to be happy. I highly recommend this game to all young married couples.

Another practical idea that can prevent much tragedy is an agreement on the part of both that neither will make a major purchase without consulting the other. The purpose of consulting is to reach agreement regarding the purchase. The term *major purchase* must be given a dollar value. For example, the couple might agree that neither would ever buy anything that costs more than $100 without such agreement. It is true that many golf clubs and lamps would still be in the showroom if couples followed this principle. But it is also true that many couples would be far happier.

Who Keeps the Books?

The final suggestion I wish to make is that you decide before marriage who will keep the books after you are married. The one who "keeps the books" is the one who pays the monthly bills and keeps tabs on the online accounts. This is the person who seeks to keep the two of you on track with the spending plan upon which you have agreed. This does not mean that the one chosen to keep the books is in charge of making financial decisions. Such decisions are to be made as a team.

The bookkeeper may not necessarily remain bookkeeper forever. For one reason or another, you may decide after the first six months that it will be far wiser if the other partner would become the bookkeeper. As a couple discusses financial details, it will usually be obvious which one is more adept at such matters.

However, be certain that the one who is not keeping the books knows how to do so and has full knowledge regarding various checking and savings accounts. Remember you are a team and both team members must be fully aware of financial details.

It is my desire that the ideas I have shared in this chapter will help the two of you fully discuss and find agreement on the financial plan you will follow once you are married. I wish someone had told me that we needed a financial plan before we got married. I think I would have followed the advice.

Talking It Over

1. What is your present financial plan? (How do you use your money?) Be as detailed as possible. If you are contemplating marriage, ask your dating partner to do the same.
2. Do you give away 10 percent of your income?
3. Do you place at least 10 percent of your income into some savings or investment plan?
4. Discuss items 2 and 3 with your prospective mate and agree on what you will do after you are married.
5. Begin doing individually whatever you plan to do after you are married. That is, if you agree to put 10 percent of your income into savings after marriage, begin to do so while you are single. (What you do now is a good indicator of how well you will follow the plan after marriage.)
6. If engaged, declare your total assets and liabilities to your fiancé. Take a realistic look at your debts and resources.
7. Together work out a payment schedule for any debts you will have when you are married.
8. Together work out a financial plan for spending your money after you are married. This will require information regarding housing and utility costs.
9. Discuss and seek agreement that neither of you will ever make a major purchase without consulting the other. No agreement—no purchase! (Agree on the dollar value of a "major purchase.")
10. Who will keep the books? Why?

9

I Wish I Had Known . . .

That mutual sexual FULFILLMENT *is not* AUTOMATIC

This was another area of marriage in which I never anticipated problems. I was fully male; she was fully female—and we had a high level of sexual attraction for each other. What more could we need? I anticipated that this part of marriage was going to be heaven for both of us. After the wedding, I discovered that what is heavenly for one may be hell for the other.

No one told me that males and females are different. To be sure, I knew the obvious physiological differences, but I knew almost nothing about female sexuality. I thought she would enjoy it as much as I did; that she would want to do it as often as I did; and that what pleasured me would also pleasure her. I repeat: I knew almost nothing about female sexuality. And I discovered that she knew little about male sexuality.

Had I done any reading on the topic, I would have discovered that the ancient Hebrew scriptures were correct when they suggested that it would take one year for the newly married couple to learn how to have mutual sexual satisfaction.[1] Again, I had been blindsided by my lack of information. What I am going to share with you in this chapter is what I wish I had known about sex before I got married.

First, I wish I had known that while men focus on intercourse, women focus on relationship. If the relationship has been fractured by harsh words or irresponsible behavior, the female will find it very hard to be interested in sex. To her, sex is an intimate act and grows out of a loving relationship. Ironically, men often think that sexual intercourse will solve whatever relationship problems may exist. One wife said, "He speaks to me with intense anger. Thirty minutes later, he says he is sorry and asks me if we can make love. He says, 'Let me show you how much I love you.' He thinks that having sex will make everything right. Well, he's wrong. I can't have sex with a man who has verbally abused me."

For a husband to expect his wife to warm up to a sexual experience after there's been an altercation in their relationship is to expect the impossible. Sincere apologies and genuine forgiveness must precede the experience of "making love."

"If I had known that taking out the garbage was sexy for my wife, I would have been taking out the garbage twice a day."

Another way of expressing this reality is that for women, sex begins in the kitchen, not in the bedroom. If he speaks her love language in the kitchen, she is far more open to having sex when they reach the bedroom. If her love language is *acts of service*, then washing dishes and taking out the garbage may be a sexual turn-on for her. I remember the husband who said to me, "If I had known that taking out the garbage was sexy for my wife, I would have been taking out the garbage twice a day. No one ever told me that."

On the other hand, if *words of affirmation* is her love language, then complimenting her on a meal or on how beautiful she looks will stir inside of her the desire to be sexually intimate with him. The same principle is true whatever the love language of your spouse. While a husband may have a satisfying sexual experience with his wife even when his "love tank" is not full, the wife would find that extremely difficult.

Second, I wish I had known that to the wife, *foreplay* is more important than the actual act of intercourse itself. While women like to simmer, men tend to reach the boiling point much faster. It is the tender touches and kisses of foreplay that bring her to the point of desiring intercourse. If the husband rushes to the finish line, she is left feeling, "What was supposed to be so special about this?" Without sufficient foreplay, the wife will often feel violated. One wife said, "I want to feel loved. All he is interested in is having intercourse."

Third, I wish I had known that mutual sexual satisfaction does not require simultaneous climax. Largely because of modern movies, many couples enter marriage with the idea that "every time we have intercourse, we will have simultaneous climax and it will be heaven for both of us." The fact is, seldom do couples have a simultaneous climax or orgasm. What is important is that each of you experiences the pleasure of climax or orgasm. Such pleasure does not have to come simultaneously. In fact, many wives indicate that they much prefer to reach orgasm as a part of foreplay. When his stimulation of the clitoris gives her the pleasure of orgasm, she is now ready for him to complete the act of intercourse and experience the pleasure of climax. The unrealistic expectation of simultaneous climax has produced unnecessary anxiety for many couples.

Fourth, I wish I had known that when one forces a particular sexual act upon one's spouse, it ceases to be an act of love and becomes sexual abuse. True love is always seeking to bring pleasure to the spouse. It is never demanding something that the spouse finds objectionable. If the two of you disagree on a particular kind of sexual expression, then it calls for communication and negotiation. If you cannot reach an agreement, then love respects the desires of the spouse who objects. To violate this principle is to sabotage mutual sexual fulfillment.

Fifth, I wish I had known that sex is more than intercourse. By its very nature, sex is a bonding experience. It is the union of male and female in the most intimate way. It is not simply the joining of two bodies. It is the union of body, soul, and spirit. I think that is why the Christian faith and most other world religions reserve intercourse for marriage. It is designed to be *the* unique bonding experience that unites a husband and wife in a lifelong intimate relationship. If intercourse is viewed only as a way to relieve sexual tension or to experience a moment of sexual pleasure, it ceases to reach its designed purpose. And it eventually becomes a mundane act of selfishness. On the other hand, when intercourse is viewed as an act of love that expresses in the deepest possible way our commitment to each other, it leads to mutual sexual fulfillment.

Sixth, I wish I had known that communication is the key that unlocks sexual fulfillment. In a culture that is saturated with explicit sex talk, I am constantly amazed at the couples who enter my counseling office who have never learned to talk about this part of their marriage. If they have tried to talk, it has often come across as condemnation and rejection. They have focused more on *telling* than they have on *listening*. The only way we can learn what is pleasurable or objectionable to the other is to listen as they choose to talk. None of us is a mind reader. That is why I've spent a great deal of my life encouraging couples to learn how to listen with empathy.

"What could I do or not do that would make the sexual part of the marriage better for you?"

Empathetic listening is listening with a view to discovering what the other person is thinking and feeling. What are their desires and frustrations? I have often encouraged young couples to ask this question once a month for the first six months of their marriage: "What could I do or not do that would make the sexual part of the marriage better for you?" Write down their answer and take it seriously. If you do this the first six months of the marriage, you will be on the road to finding mutual sexual fulfillment.

Number seven, I wish I had known that the past never remains in the past. In today's sexually open culture, many couples have been sexually active before marriage. The commonly held idea is that sexual experience before marriage better prepares you for marriage. All of the research indicates otherwise. In fact, the divorce rate among those who have had previous sexual experience is twice as high as those who have had no sexual experience before marriage.[2] The reality is that previous sexual experience often becomes a psychological barrier in achieving sexual unity in marriage.

Our culture has taught that sex before marriage is recreational and that once you get married, you can simply wipe the slate clean, commit yourself to be sexually faithful to your spouse, and all will go well. However, it is not that easy to wipe the psychological slate clean. Couples often struggle with the desire to know their spouse's sexual history, and when they know, it sometimes becomes a memory that is difficult to erase. When it comes to marriage, something deep within the human psyche cries out for an exclusive relationship. And we are pained by the thought that our spouse has been sexually intimate with others.

I believe it is far better to deal with past sexual experiences before marriage. When we are silent on this subject and enter marriage without discussing our past sexual activities, almost always the past has a way of erupting into the present. When this happens after marriage, the awareness of deception is often more difficult to overcome than the sexual activity itself.

If knowing the truth about past sexual experiences does not help you find healing and acceptance before marriage, then my advice is to postpone the marriage while the two of you work through the issue with each other or perhaps with the help of a counselor. If ultimately you cannot find healing and acceptance of the past, then in my opinion you would be wise to cancel your plans to get married. If you are struggling with this issue, I would encourage you to read *The Invisible Bond: How to Break Free from Your Sexual Past,*[3] which will give you further help on how to process the past in a positive way.

I hope that the ideas I have shared in this chapter will help you enter marriage with a much more realistic view of how to find mutual sexual fulfillment. I have one final suggestion. During the first year of your marriage, read and discuss with each other a book on marital sex. You will find some suggested books in the resource section at the end of this book.

Talking It Over

1. How would you describe the current cultural perspective on sex?
2. In what ways do you agree or disagree with this perspective?
3. Research indicates that couples who have sexual intercourse before marriage have a higher divorce rate than those who do not. Why do you think this would be true?
4. To what degree have you shared your sexual history with the person you are dating?
5. If you are seriously contemplating marriage, you may want to read *The Gift of Sex* by Clifford and Joyce Penner.[4]

10

I Wish I Had Known . . .

That I was MARRYING *into a* FAMILY

If you think that after the wedding it will just be the two of you, your thinking is wrong. You are marrying into a family, for better or for worse. Her family does not disappear the day after the wedding. Both of your parents may allow you to have a few days for a honeymoon alone but after that, they will expect to be a part of your lives. In some non-Western cultures, parental involvement is more pronounced and overt. In some cases, the bride actually moves into the house with her husband and his parents and lives there indefinitely. After all, the dowry was paid, and she belongs to his family. His mother will teach her how to be the wife he needs. In Western culture, in-law relationships are not rigidly formalized but are nonetheless real.

For over thirty years, couples have sat in my office and made the following complaints:

- "His mother wants to tell me how to cook. I've been cooking for ten years. I don't need her help."
- "Her father doesn't like me. He tells his friends that his daughter married down. I guess he wanted me to be a doctor or a lawyer. I don't have the heart to tell him that as a plumber, I am making more money than either one of them."
- "His sister and his mother never include me in their social activities. They invite his brother's wife, but they never invite me."
- "Her brother is addicted to sports. We don't have much in common. I don't think he has read a book in years and he has no interest in politics."
- "Her father is an accountant. Every time we are together, he's giving me advice on how to manage our money. Frankly, I don't usually agree with his advice, but I try to be nice."
- "My husband's brother is always telling him what he should do. He is four years older than my husband. I guess he's still trying to be the big brother, but it bothers me that my husband is so influenced by his brother's advice. If I have a different idea, he always sides with his brother."
- "My wife's parents give her money to buy things we can't afford. I resent that. I wish they would let us run our own lives."
- "My husband's parents just drop in unannounced and expect us to drop everything and visit with them. It's beginning to be very irritating. I don't want to hurt their feelings, but I wish they would call and find out if it is a convenient time for them to visit."

When you marry, you become a part of an extended family. This family may include a mother, a father, a stepmother, a stepfather, brothers, sisters, stepbrothers and stepsisters, uncles, aunts, cousins, nieces, nephews, stepchildren, and perhaps an ex-husband or an ex-wife. You cannot ignore this extended family. They will not go away. Your relationship may be distant or close, positive or negative, but you will have a relationship because you are marrying into a family.

Life will be much easier if you can have a positive relationship with this extended family. Your relationship with each of these individuals depends on the opportunities you have to interact with each other. If you live a thousand miles from both of your extended families, then your relationship may be positive but distant. Your opportunities to develop your relationship may be limited to holidays, weddings, and funerals. However, if you live in closer proximity, then you may have a great deal of interaction with members of your extended family.

Five Key Issues

Normally, the most intimate of these relationships will be with your spouse's parents. Thus, in this chapter, I want to focus on mother-in-law and father-in-law relationships. What then are the issues that will need to be processed with your in-laws? Here are five typical areas that will call for understanding and negotiation.

One of the first issues that will likely demand your attention is holidays. At the top of the list will be Christmas. In Western culture, more families get together at Christmas than at any other holiday. Often, the problem is that his parents want both of you at their house on Christmas Day and her parents want the same. If they both live in the same town, that may be possible. If they live in the same state, it could be Christmas Eve at one set of parents and Christmas Day with the other. However, if they live several states away, you may have to negotiate Christmas with his parents this year and her parents next year, and spend Thanksgiving with the parent or parents who won't see you at Christmas. There may be other holidays that will be deemed extremely important for one or both of your families.

> Unless you have spent a great deal of time with in-laws before marriage, you may be blindsided by these expectations.

In addition to holidays, there will also be traditions. One young wife said, "My sister and I have always taken our mother out for dinner on her birthday. Now that we are married, my husband says we don't have the money for me to fly back for Mom's birthday. I'm finding this really hard to accept. I don't want my mother and sister to feel badly toward him, but I'm afraid that's what will happen." A young husband said, "For as long as I can remember, on the Fourth of July, my family has a fish fry. The men go fishing early in the morning. It's an all-day event. It's the one time each year that I get to see all of my cousins. My wife thinks that we should spend the day with her parents, but all they do is go out to a restaurant for the evening meal. We could do that any time." Traditions are often undergirded by deep emotions and should never be treated lightly.

Your in-laws will also have expectations. Unless you have spent a great deal of time with them before marriage, you may be blindsided by these expectations. One husband said, "I found out the hard way that when my wife and I go out to a restaurant with her parents, they expect to pay for our meal one time and they expect me to pay for it the next time. I was so embarrassed when my wife said, 'It's your time to pay.' When we go out with my parents, they always pay for our meal. It had never crossed my mind that they were expecting me to pay."

Some of these expectations will have religious overtones. A young wife said, "I found out that when we spend the weekend with his parents, they expect us to go to the synagogue with them on Friday nights even though both of us are Christians. I feel very uncomfortable but I don't want to hurt their feelings. I'm wondering if, when they come to visit us, they will go to church with us on Sunday." Her husband said, "When we go to visit her folks for a weekend, they expect me to wear a suit when I go to church with them on Sunday morning. We attend a contemporary church and I only have one suit that I bought for my grandmother's funeral five years ago. I feel uncomfortable wearing it."

Each of your in-laws may also have patterns of behavior that you find irritating or troublesome. You may discover that your father-in-law goes out with "the boys" every Thursday night and normally comes home intoxicated and verbally abuses his wife. Your mother-in-law tells your wife about this behavior; she tells you. You wish there was something you could do but you feel helpless. You are troubled by your father-in-law's behavior but you are also irritated that every time your wife talks to her mother, she brings up the topic, and your wife gets upset.

Megan had been married only five months when she said in the counseling office, "My mother-in-law is the most organized woman I know. You should see her closets. Every shoe is in the right place and all of her dresses are color coordinated. The problem is I'm not very organized and when she comes to our apartment, she tries to give me suggestions that she thinks will make my life easier. I'm sorry but that's just not who I am. Besides that,

I don't have time to keep everything organized."

Your in-laws may also have strongly held religious beliefs that differ from yours. One young husband said, "Every time I'm around her father, it's like he's trying to convert me to his brand of Christianity. I am a Christian but I'm not as dogmatic and pushy as he is. I think religion is a personal matter and I resent him trying to pressure me to agree with him."

Suzanne, who grew up in a Lutheran home, said, "His folks are Baptist and are constantly talking about my getting baptized. I was baptized as a baby and I don't feel any need to be re-baptized. They act like it is a big deal. I don't get it."

Learning to Listen

In these and numerous other areas, you will discover that your in-laws are individuals who have unique thoughts, feelings, and desires. These may differ from your own thoughts, feelings, and desires. So, how do you build a positive relationship with your in-laws? I want to suggest that the process begins by learning to listen empathetically. By empathetic listening, I mean listening with a view to understanding what your in-laws think, how they came to that conclusion, and how strongly they feel about it.

"Every time I'm around her father, it's like he's trying to convert me to his brand of Christianity."

By nature, most of us are not good listeners. We often listen long enough to give a rebuttal and we end up in needless arguments. Empathetic listening holds judgment until you are certain that you understand what the other person is saying. This involves asking clarifying questions such as, "What I understand you to be saying is . . . Is that correct?" or, "It sounds like you are asking me to . . . Is that what you want?" Once you have listened long enough to clearly understand what they are saying and how strongly they feel about it, you are then free to give your perspective on the subject. Because you have listened to them without condemnation, they are far more likely to hear your honest perspective.

Empathetic listening does not require you to agree with the other person's ideas, but it does require you to treat them and their ideas with respect. If you respect their ideas and speak to them with kindness, they are far more likely to respect your ideas and treat you kindly. Mutual understanding and mutual respect grows out of empathetic listening.

When communicating with in-laws, always speak for yourself. Instead of saying, "You hurt my feelings when you said that," you might say, "I felt hurt when I heard you say that." When you start your sentence with "I," you are giving your perspective. When you begin your sentence with "you," you are placing blame and will likely experience a defensive response from your in-laws. The husband who says, "I feel frustrated when Kimberly tells me that every time you talk you mention your husband's problem with alcohol and verbal abuse. I'm wondering if you want us to do something and if so, what do you think we could do?" will likely open the door to a meaningful conversation.

Learning to Negotiate

The third ingredient to having good relationships with your in-laws is learning to negotiate differences. Negotiation begins by someone making a proposal. Jeremy said to his wife's parents, "I know that you would like for us to be here for Christmas Day and celebrate with the family. My parents, of course, have the same desire. Because you are 500 miles apart, we know that we can't be at both places on the same day. I'm wondering about alternating between Thanksgiving and Christmas. We could be with you guys this Christmas and with my folks on Thanksgiving. And next year, we would reverse the order. I'm just trying to find something that will work for both families."

Negotiation is enhanced when you make requests and not demands.

Jeremy has made a proposal. Now his in-laws have the opportunity to accept the proposal or to modify the proposal or to make a different proposal of their own. It is the process of listening and respecting each other's ideas that allows the process of negotiation to go forward. Eventually, you reach a solution that everyone can agree with and the relationship with your in-laws is strengthened.

Differences regarding holidays, traditions, expectations, patterns of behavior, and religion all call for negotiation. The ancient Hebrew scriptures observed, "How good and pleasant it is when brothers live together in unity."[1] Unity requires negotiation.

Negotiation is enhanced when you make requests and not demands. Tim said to his parents, "We really enjoy you guys coming over and we want to spend time with you, though I would like to make a request. Instead of just stopping by, would it be possible for you to call and see if it is a good evening for us? The reason I ask is that last week when you stopped by on Thursday night, I ended up staying up until midnight trying to get my report ready for work the next day. Friday night would have been a much better night for me. Does that make sense and is that possible?"

Tim has made a proposal and a request. His parents may agree with his request; they may show resistance to his request; or they may make an alternate proposal, such as agreeing upon a particular night that they will normally come unless there is a specific reason to move it to another night. At any rate, by making a request and not a demand, Tim has kept the relationship positive.

Learning Their Love Language

My final suggestion for maintaining good and positive in-law relationships is to learn the primary love language of your in-laws and speak that language regularly. When your in-laws feel genuinely loved, it creates a positive climate in which to negotiate differences. Nothing communicates love more deeply than speaking the right love language. If you don't know the love language of your in-laws, you might give them a copy of my book *The Five Love Languages: The Secret to Love that Lasts.* Once they have read the book and understand the concept, they may want to discuss their primary love languages. You can also share your love languages with them. When families effectively communicate love, they create positive in-law relationships.

Neither Karolyn nor I experienced a great deal of trauma in relating to our extended families. The first two years of our marriage, we lived two thousand miles from both of our families. Christmas was our only time at home and both families lived in the same town. My family celebrated on Christmas Eve and her family on Christmas Day. Therefore, in-law relationships were distant but positive.

Karolyn's father was deceased before we got married. When I finished graduate studies and we moved closer to our families, her mother was my chief cheerleader. Her love language was *acts of service.* After I painted the house for her, I could do no wrong. My parents were helpful, positive, and never overbearing. I certainly would not have been prepared to deal with in-law conflicts. Karolyn and I never discussed the subject. I realize now how naïve we were. The hundreds of couples who have walked through my counseling office have made me realize that we were the exception. Having good in-law relationships normally requires time and effort.

I'm hoping that this chapter will help the two of you surface potential areas of conflict with your extended families and to talk about how you will handle these issues. The more thoroughly you do this before marriage, the less likely you are to be blindsided once you are married.

Talking It Over

1. Share with each other how your families typically celebrate Christmas and other significant holidays. Look for potential areas of conflict.

2. What are the strongly held traditions in each of your families? These traditions may not focus on birthdays or holidays, but they are extremely important to your family members.

3. Seek to discover the expectations that your in-laws may have of each of you after marriage. If you have siblings or friends who are married, you might discuss with them the kind of expectations they have encountered from parents and in-laws.

4. Like the rest of us, all in-laws have certain patterns of behavior they follow. Some of these are positive, such as playing golf on Saturdays. Others are negative, such as getting drunk on Thursday nights. What patterns do you observe in each of your parents? Share these with each other and talk about those things that you might find irritating.

5. What are the strongly held religious beliefs of your parents? Share these with each other and talk about areas in which you might feel uncomfortable.

6. When your parents are discussing ideas with which you disagree, how well have you learned to withhold judgment and listen empathetically so that you can make an intelligent response? Share with each other illustrations of times in which you have listened well or not so well.

7. In your normal conversations, how well have you learned to speak for yourself? When the two of you have a disagreement, how often do you start your sentences with the word *you* as opposed to *I*? Discuss this with each other and focus on learning to speak for yourself.

8. When two people disagree, it calls for negotiation. The process requires someone to make a proposal, listen to a counterproposal, and seek to find a solution that everyone can agree on. How well have you done this in the past? Share your memories with each other.

9. Negotiation is enhanced when you make *requests* rather than *demands*. Think of times in which your requests have sounded like demands to the other person. Ask each other how you might reframe your desire so that it sounds like a request.

10. Do you know the primary love language of each of your parents? Do you know the love language of your in-laws? If so, how well are you speaking their love language? If not, what will you do to make this discovery?

11. If the person you are thinking of marrying already has children, I highly recommend that you read and discuss the book

The Smart Step-Family[2] by Ron Deal. The number one conflict in marriages that involve children is the conflict between child and stepparent.

11

I Wish I Had Known . . .

That **SPIRITUALITY** *is not to be equated with* **"GOING TO CHURCH"**

Nine months after the wedding, Jill and Matt sat in my office. Jill said, "We've got a problem and we don't know how to solve it." "So, what's the problem?" I inquired. "Matt doesn't want to go to church with me anymore. He says that church is boring and that he feels closer to God on the golf course than he does in church. So for the last month, he drives off to the golf course while I drive off to church. It just doesn't seem right to me. I never dreamed that this would happen.

"Before we got married, Matt went to church with me every Sunday. He always seemed to like it. We discussed the sermons. He told me that he was a Christian, but how can you be a Christian and not want to go to church? He says that I'm judging him and maybe I am. But I'm deeply hurt and I'm beginning to feel that maybe we made a mistake by getting married."

For Jill, the issue seemed to be attending church versus not attending church. However, Matt had a totally different perspective on spirituality. He did not grow up attending church. While a student at the university, he had become involved in a student-led Christian organization. After several months of attending meetings, and reading the Bible and other Christian books, he had come to consider himself a Christian. While he and Jill were dating, he attended church with her every Sunday and found it interesting. But now that he was out of college and working full-time, he found the church services to be much too predictable and did not find the sermons to be very helpful. He sincerely felt closer to God on the golf course than he did at church. He could not understand why attending church was such a big deal for Jill.

On the other hand, Jill was devastated. Attending church with other Christians was one of the tenets of her faith. It was unthinkable that a good Christian would not go to church. "What will we do when we have children?" she asked. "I can't bear the thought of my children not going to church." I could tell that Matt was getting frustrated. "Jill, we don't have children," he said. "We can cross that bridge when we get there."

Many couples never get around to discussing their religious beliefs at all.

Matt and Jill were one of many couples who have sat in my office over the years and shared their conflicts over their religious beliefs. And yet, spirituality is often the last thing to be discussed in a dating relationship. In fact, many couples never get around to discussing their religious beliefs at all. As a counselor, I find this extremely disappointing.

Since I hold undergraduate and graduate degrees in anthropology, I am often drawn to the cultural discoveries that have been made by anthropologists. One of those discoveries is that man is incurably religious. There are no cultures that have not developed a system of beliefs about the nonmaterial world. From the Roman veneration of mythical gods to the belief in evil spirits found in aboriginal tribes, man believes there is more than can be seen by the eye. The second discovery of the anthropologist is that these religious beliefs greatly influence the behavior of those who believe them. This is true both in what is often called primitive religions and also in the more advanced religions such as Judaism, Christianity, Buddhism, Hinduism, and Islam. Our view of spirituality greatly influences the way we live our lives.

Therefore, when couples are contemplating marriage, religion needs to be near the top of the list in matters that need to be discussed. The question is, "Are our spiritual beliefs compatible?" or, "Are we marching to the beat of the same drummer?" Few things have the potential for causing marital conflict more than divergent spiritual views. That is why most world religions encourage their adherents to marry within their own religious tradition. In the Christian faith, the scriptures admonish, "Do not be yoked together with unbelievers. For what do righteousness and wickedness have in common? Or what fellowship can light have with darkness? What harmony is there between Christ and Belial? What does a believer have in common with an unbeliever? What agreement is there between the temple of God and idols?"[1] These are cogent questions and the wise couple will not avoid them.

What Do You Think about God?

So what are the issues that need to be looked at? First, there is one's *concept of God.* The Hebrew scriptures begin with these words: "In the beginning God created the heavens and the earth."[2] A few paragraphs later we read, "So God created human beings in his own image, in the image of God he created them; male and female he created them."[3] Are these words to be taken literally? Is there a transcendent, powerful creator who not only created the universe but made man in His own image? Or is this simply to be taken as Hebrew mythology? Your answer to those questions will have a profound impact on your self-perception and how you live your life. If you agree that God exists as the creator and sustainer of the universe, the next question is "Has God spoken?" The Christian scriptures affirm, "In the past God spoke to our forefathers through the prophets at many times and in various ways, but in these last days he has spoken to us by his Son, whom he appointed heir of all things, and through whom he made the universe. The Son is the radiance of God's glory and the exact representation of his being, sustaining all things by his powerful word. After he had provided purification for sins, he sat down at the right hand of the Majesty in heaven."[4] Thus, the Christian belief is that God has spoken through the ancient Hebrew prophets, recorded in the Old Testament scriptures, and that Jesus Christ is the prophesied Messiah, the Son of God, who would pay the penalty for man's wrongdoing so that God could forgive mankind and still be a just God. That is why Christians invite all to accept Christ as their Messiah and receive God's forgiveness and enter a love relationship with God.

Your answers to the following questions will reveal the level of your spiritual compatibility. Is there a God who created the universe and made man in His image? Has that God spoken? If so, how has He spoken? What has He said and how have I responded to His message? These are fundamental questions that need to be answered honestly.

It has been my observation that many people come to adulthood never having explored their own spiritual belief system. They call themselves Buddhist, Hindu, or Christian but they do so simply because they were raised in a Buddhist, Hindu, or Christian home. They are cultural Buddhists, Hindus, or Christians. Personally, they have not explored the fundamental beliefs of those religions. We do not choose our family, and thus, the religion, into which we are born. But as adults, we have the responsibility to seek truth in all areas of life. If you realize that your religion is simply a cultural artifact, I would encourage you to take the time to explore the history and beliefs of your religious heritage and discuss your journey openly with the person you are dating. If you cannot be honest and open about your religious beliefs before marriage, you are not likely to do so after marriage and your religious beliefs will likely become a source of conflict.

Exploring the Branches

Inasmuch as 80 percent of the population of the United States claims Christianity as their religion and inasmuch as this is my own personal religious heritage, let me explore with my Christian readers additional issues that I think need to be addressed before the decision to marry. We all know that within the universal Christian church, Christians come in many flavors. The three major branches of Christendom are Eastern Orthodoxy, Roman Catholicism, and Protestantism. While these three agree on certain core beliefs, such as the divinity of Christ, His sacrificial death, and His resurrection from the dead, they disagree on many other issues. If you are contemplating marriage to someone outside your own Christian tradition, I urge you to explore both of your traditions and seek to negotiate your differences. To marry simply because you are "in love" and to ignore the implications of these spiritual differences are signs of immaturity.

Assuming that both of you are members of the same Christian tradition, it is time to examine the finer points of belief and practice. Within the Orthodox tradition, there are Greek Orthodox, Russian Orthodox, Armenian Orthodox, etc. All of these have beliefs and practices that differ from country to country. Within the Roman Catholic Church, beliefs and practices also differ from country to country and often within the same country. For example, more recently in America there has been a strong charismatic movement among Roman Catholics. Within the Protestant tradition, there are many denominations: Lutheran, Presbyterian, Baptist, and Methodists to name just a few. And there are a whole group of churches that call themselves nondenominational. There is great diversity in beliefs and practices within these various Protestant groups. These differences need to be fully explored if you are contemplating marriage.

To marry simply because you are "in love" and to ignore the implications of these spiritual differences is a sign of immaturity.

What Kind of "Christian"?

Thus far, I have been talking about theological differences in faith and practice, but now let me turn to the personal side. We clearly recognize that there are different levels of commitment among Christians. For example, some people who call themselves Christians attend church only during the Easter and Christmas holidays. Other than those holidays, their religion tends to influence them very little. On the other hand, there are many who attend church on a regular basis. For some, it is a once-a-week event that lasts for one hour to three hours, depending on the format of the worship service. Others, however, are involved not only in corporate worship but are involved in small Bible-study groups that both offer spiritual support and explore how to apply the teachings of scripture to their personal lives. These people live in deep and close community with those who attend the group. They are willing to sacrifice for each other. They care enough to be honest with each other and they are often reaching out to serve the community in practical ways. Many of these Christians also have a daily devotional time in which they consciously read the scriptures to hear the voice of God and respond to God with honest questions, praise, thanksgiving, or requests for help. They view Christianity as a personal love relationship with Christ. This daily "quiet time" is the most important part of their day.

Thus, it becomes extremely important to discover what kind of Christian you are dating. What is their level of commitment and involvement in the Christian community? How important is their faith to them? And what kind of impact does it have on their personal life? It should be obvious that an Easter-Christmas Christian is very different from a daily "quiet time" Christian.

It should be obvious that an Easter-Christmas Christian is very different from a daily "quiet time" Christian.

I remember the young lady who said to me, "I've been dating Andrew for three years. When we started dating, he told me that he was a Christian. We have many common interests and we have had many wonderful times together. But I have come to realize that we are not marching to the beat of the same drummer when it comes to spirituality. For him, Christianity is a religion; something you do on Sunday but it has little relevance to how he makes decisions and lives his life. For me, Christianity is my life. Nothing is more important to me than investing my life in serving Christ. I realize that we don't have the spiritual foundation on which to build a Christian marriage. Therefore, I am breaking off our dating relationship."

I think this young lady was extremely mature. If after three years she had seen little spiritual movement on his part to become more personally involved in his relationship with God, to think that would change after marriage would be naïve. Three years later, she married a young man who had a similar level of commitment to his faith in Christ and the two of them are in the process of building a truly Christian marriage.

For many dating couples, spirituality is an unexplored topic. They simply assume that this area of life will take care of itself after marriage. Others who openly discuss matters of spirituality often ignore the warning signs. They are so in love with each other, enjoy being with each other, and can see themselves making each other happy for the rest of their lives, and they close their eyes to huge differences in their views of spirituality.

Jill and Matt, the couple we met at the beginning of this chapter, eventually discovered spiritual intimacy. After several counseling sessions in which I helped them listen to the heart of the other person and try to understand how important this issue was to them, they were able to affirm each other's concerns and become friends instead of enemies. Once they moved from an adversarial relationship to a friendship where two people were trying to understand each other and solve a conflict rather than win an argument, the resolution became rather easy.

Matt agreed to give up Sunday morning golf and began attending church with Jill. Jill agreed that she would join him in looking for a church that he would find more engaging. They found such a church, and together, they are deeply involved not only in attendance but are involved weekly in teaching a fifth-grade children's class. Incidentally, they now have a three-year-old son. Both agree that they are glad they found a meeting place in their spiritual journey before their son was born.

Religious beliefs are often accompanied by strong emotions and deeply held convictions. Even atheists often hold their non-God views tenaciously, and those beliefs affect the way they approach life. In that sense, though they deny the existence of God, they are deeply religious. Because our religious beliefs affect all of life, it is very important that we explore the foundation of spiritual compatibility before we make the commitment to marriage. I hope that this chapter will help you do that.

Talking It Over

1. What are the basic religious beliefs of your parents?
2. Where are you in your own spiritual journey? Have you accepted, rejected, or modified the religious beliefs that you were taught as a child?
3. What are your basic beliefs about God?
4. What religious organizations are you affiliated with? How active is your involvement?
5. How do your religious beliefs affect your daily lifestyle?

6. If you are considering marriage, discuss your answers with your dating partner.
7. Do you think you hold enough in common to build spiritual intimacy in your marriage?

12

I Wish I Had Known . . .

That PERSONALITY *profoundly influences* BEHAVIOR

No one questions the axiom that we are all unique. The question is, how unique? I wish I'd known that personality (those characteristics that make us unique) would profoundly affect our marriage.

Before we got married, I dreamed about how wonderful it would be to get up every morning and have breakfast with my wife. After we got married, I found out that Karolyn didn't do mornings. Breakfast was not her "thing." Upon reflection I did remember that during the dating years, she told me, "Don't call me in the mornings. I'm not responsible for what I say or do before noon." I took it as a joke and laughed. I never called her in the morning because I was busy "doing my own thing." After marriage I discovered that she was serious. My dream of a quiet romantic breakfast with my wife was shattered in the first month of our marriage. I was left to eat breakfast in silence, except for the songs the birds were singing outside the window.

On the other hand, before we got married Karolyn had visions of what the two of us would do between 10 p.m. and midnight. Her visions included reading and discussing books, watching movies together, playing intellectually stimulating games, and discussing the deeper issues of life. What she did not know was that my physical, emotional, and intellectual motor shut down at 10 p.m. The possibility of my carrying on an intelligent conversation was greatly diminished after that hour. It is true that while we were dating, I stayed alive and engaged with her until midnight. But I was pushed along by euphoric feelings of "being in love." The excitement of being with her and doing things together kept the adrenalin flowing, and she had no idea that this would not continue after we were married.

Neither of us knew before marriage that there are "morning persons" and there are "night persons." Morning persons awake with the enthusiasm of a kangaroo, springing to face the day with excitement, while the night person hides under the covers and thinks, "They must be playing a game—no one can be that excited in the morning." Night persons have their "prime time" from 10 p.m. until . . . That's when they enjoy reading, painting, playing games, doing anything that demands a lot of energy, while the morning person is quickly fading at that hour.

This personality difference may have a profound impact upon the couple's sexual relationship. The morning person wants to go to bed at ten, cuddle, and make love, while the night person is saying, "You have got to be kidding. I can't go to bed this early." The morning person may feel rejected, while the night person feels like they are being controlled. This may well lead to arguments and frustration. Is there hope for this couple?

Certainly, if they choose to respect their differences and negotiate a solution. For example, the night person may agree to have sex at 10 p.m. if the morning person will allow them to leave the bedroom after love-making and pursue their other interests until midnight. However, if the morning person insists that the night person remain in bed after making love, that person may feel manipulated, controlled, and frustrated. A morning person will never become a night person, and a night person will never become a morning person. It's a part of our personality. With effort, we can push ourselves to be functional in those early or late hours that are not prime time for us. But it will never come without effort.

A morning person will never become a night person, and a night person will never become a morning person.

If Karolyn and I had known that I was a morning person and she was a night person, and if we had used our dating time to discuss this personality difference, we would have saved ourselves a lot of emotional pain. I would not have felt rejected because she was not having breakfast with me, and she would not have felt controlled by my insisting that she go to bed at 10 p.m. Yes, I wish we had known that personality differences profoundly influence behavior.

Half Full or Half Empty?

Let's look at some of the other personality differences that often go undiscovered and undiscussed before marriage. The pessimist and the optimist are often attracted to each other. The optimist

> In the dating stage of the relationship, we each assume that the other person views the world as we view it.

sees the glass as half full; the pessimist sees it as half empty. The optimist sees the possibilities while the pessimist sees the problems. Each of us has a basic leaning in one direction or the other, but we are often unaware of this aspect of our personality.

In the dating stage of the relationship, we each assume that the other person views the world as we view it. Because we are each enamored with the other and seeking to accommodate each other, this personality difference may not be apparent. For example, the optimist tends to be a risk taker because he is convinced in his own mind that everything will turn out fine. Thus, he may suggest that the two of them go bungee jumping. The pessimist by nature does not want to take risks because she assumes that the worst could happen. Therefore, she would never have entertained the thought of bungee jumping, but because she admires and trusts her lover, she is willing to do something she would never have done on her own. The optimist is thrilled to be dating someone who is willing to be adventuresome, while never realizing that she has gone far beyond her emotional comfort zone.

Two years after marriage when he suggests that the two of them go rock climbing, she strongly resists the idea. Not only is she unwilling, she also resists the idea of him going alone or with friends. She can envision herself being a widow and cannot understand why he would be willing to take such a risk. On the other hand, he is totally blown away by her response. He wonders what happened to her spirit of adventure. Why is she being such a killjoy?

Because they failed to discover and discuss this personality difference before marriage, they find themselves embroiled in a conflict that neither of them understands. In reality, they are both simply being who they are, an optimist and a pessimist. The problem is neither of them knew who the other person was before they got married. The euphoria of the dating experience blinded them to this personality difference. Had they discussed this difference before marriage, he would have realized that she would never be a rock climber, nor would she ever go skydiving with him. He would also have realized that if he chose to do such things, he would do so in the face of great resistance from his wife.

This personality difference is likely to create conflicts in the area of money management. The optimist will tend to be an adventurous investor, willing to take huge levels of risk with the hope of positive results. On the other hand, the pessimist will want to invest in more stable and secure markets. They will spend sleepless nights if the spouse pulls them into a high-risk investment. And if the investment goes south, the pessimist will blame the optimist for taking undue risks with their money. The optimist is likely to see the pessimist as being non-supportive of their ideas and thus, blame the spouse for "holding them back" from success.

The answer to this personality difference lies in understanding and accepting the differences, and not condemning each other for being who they are. They must then negotiate a method of honoring each other's personality. One such plan may be to agree on a dollar amount that the couple would have in secure investments before the optimist would engage in high-risk investments. Once this minimum level of investments is in place, they could agree on a dollar amount that he could invest in a higher-risk investment with the understanding that if he lost it all, she would not condemn him. On the other hand, if the investment is successful, she commends him for his investment skills and together they celebrate their financial success.

If a dating couple is willing to negotiate these kinds of arrangements before they get married, they will save themselves many unnecessary arguments over how they will handle the finances. The same principle is true in scores of other areas in which the pessimist and the optimist are likely to have very different views about the action that should be taken. Understanding, accepting, and negotiating personality differences are essential in building a foundation for a healthy marriage.

Neatniks and Slobs

Then there are the Neatnik and the Slob. "I've never known anyone as sloppy as Ben," said Alicia. How many wives have said this about their husbands less than a year after their wedding? Interestingly, before marriage this never bothered Alicia. Oh, she may have noticed that the car was sometimes messy or that his apartment was not as neat as she would have had it, but somehow she concluded that "Ben is a more relaxed person than I am. That's good; I like that. I need to loosen up a little." Ben, on the other hand, looked at Alicia and found an angel. "Isn't it wonderful that Alicia is always so tidy? Now I don't have to worry about keeping everything clean because she will take care of that." However, three years later he is being bombarded with verbal stones of condemnation to which he responds, "I don't understand why you would get so upset over a few dishes left out."

Some people do live by the motto "A place for everything and everything in its place." Other people have no compulsion to put away their tools, clothes, used coffee mugs, or anything else. After all, they may use them again in a week or two. They reason, "Why would you want to waste time picking up dirty clothes every day? Leave them on the floor until it's time to wash them. They aren't going anywhere and they don't bother me."

Yes, we are wired differently and have difficulty understanding why the other person would not see it our way. This personality difference is not hard to discover; it simply requires that during the dating time you keep your eyes open to reality. Look at his car and his apartment and you will know whether he is a Neatnik or a Slob. Look at her kitchen and her bedroom closet and you will also know which personality pattern is natural for her. If the two of you fall into the same category, you will either have an immaculate home or a place where you have to step over the clutter. But both of you will be happy. If you fall into different categories, then now is the time for negotiation. Face reality and discuss who will be responsible for what after you are married in order to keep some level of emotional sanity. If she is willing to pick up his dirty clothes daily and put them in the laundry hamper as his mother did when he was in high school, this is fine. However, if she expects him to be more responsible, then he must be willing to change or else hire his mother to come over daily to pick up his clothes. Certainly a satisfactory solution can be negotiated—but the time to start negotiation is before marriage.

When the Dead Sea Weds a Babbling Brook

Another area of personality differences is related to speech. Some people talk freely about everything. Others are more thoughtful, introspective, and less likely to share their thoughts and feelings. I have often referred to the latter as the "Dead Sea" and the former as the "Babbling Brook." In the nation of Israel, the Dead Sea receives waters from the Jordan River. But the Dead Sea goes nowhere. Many people have that kind of personality. They can receive all kinds of thoughts, feelings, and experiences throughout the day. They have a large reservoir in which they store the experiences of the day and are perfectly happy not to talk. In fact, if you say to a Dead Sea, "What's wrong? Why aren't you talking tonight?" they'll likely say, "Nothing's wrong. What makes you think something is wrong?" The Dead Sea is being perfectly honest. He or she is content not to talk.

On the other hand, the Babbling Brook is the individual for whom whatever comes into the eye gate or the ear gate comes out the mouth gate—usually in less than sixty seconds. Whatever they see, whatever they hear, they tell. In fact, if no one is at home they will call someone on the telephone and ask, "Do you know what I just heard?" They have no reservoir; whatever they experience, it spills over and they tell it to someone.

Often a Dead Sea will marry a Babbling Brook. Before marriage, the differences are viewed as attractive. For example, while dating, the Dead Sea can relax. He or she does not have to think "How will I get the conversation started?" or, "How will I keep the conversation flowing?" All they have to do is sit there, nod their head, and say, "Uh-huh." The Babbling Brook will fill up the evening. On the other hand, the Babbling Brook finds the Dead Sea equally attractive because Dead Seas are the world's best listeners. However, five years after marriage, the Babbling Brook may be saying, "We've been married five years and I don't know her." At the same time, the Dead Sea may be saying, "I know him too well. I wish he would stop the flow and give me a break."

These differences are also seen in the way people tell stories.

The Babbling Brook tends to be a *painter*. If they are telling you an experience they have had, they will paint a beautiful, detailed picture of the event. They will tell you whether it was cloudy or the sun was shining, which way the wind was blowing, what kind of flowers were in the background, and how many people were standing on the other side of the parking lot. On the other hand, the Dead Sea tends to be a *pointer*. If they were telling the same experience, it would be much shorter with fewer details. They simply "get to the point." They are bottom-line communicators. Often in a marriage, the pointer will find it very difficult to listen to the long and detailed account of the painter. They will sometimes interrupt and say "Could you just get to the point?" However, when the painter is listening to the pointer, they will often ask questions trying to glean more details so they have a better picture of the pointer's story.

The *painter* will always be a *painter* and the *pointer* will always be a *pointer*. These personality patterns of speech are not likely to change, nor is one better than another. However, if we understand these personality differences, we are less likely to try to change each other after we are married. The Dead Sea will never become a Babbling Brook. So the person who is married to a Dead Sea must be content to live with a person who will not readily share all of their thoughts and feelings. Most Dead Seas are open to questions and are willing to share more if the Babbling Brook will ask those questions. The Dead Sea is not willfully withholding information; they simply have no compulsion to share all of their thoughts, feelings, and experiences.

While the Dead Sea may be content to listen to the constant talk of the Babbling Brook, he or she may sometimes long for moments of silence. That is why they sometimes withdraw to the computer or other activities. The Babbling Brook must understand. They are not being rejected by the Dead Sea. The Dead Sea is simply longing for a more contemplative climate. When these personality differences are discussed before marriage, they are far less likely to be troublesome after marriage.

Passives and Aggressives

The old adage says, "Some people read history; others make it." Often these people are married to each other. The *aggressive* husband or wife believes that each day is a new opportunity to advance the cause. They will aggressively pursue what they want, what they believe to be right, or what they think should happen. They will go to all ends, they will turn every stone, and they will do everything humanly possible to accomplish their goals in life. On the other hand, the passive person will spend time thinking, analyzing, wondering "What if?" and waiting for something good to happen. Their theme is, "Everything comes to him who waits."

Before marriage, these traits made them seem compatible. The *aggressive partner* found it comforting to observe the calm, cool, and collected nature of the other person. They liked the stable, predictable nature of the one they loved. The *passive person* was pleased to have someone make plans and chart courses for their future. They admired the accomplishments of their aggressive lover.

After marriage, the couple often finds these traits divisive. The aggressive partner keeps trying to push the passive partner into action. "Come on; we can make this happen" is their mantra. On the other hand, the passive partner keeps saying, "Let's wait. There might be a better opportunity later. Don't get so excited. Everything is going to work out."

Are these traits observable in the dating stage of the relationship? The answer is yes, but often they are never discussed. The passive person tends to simply go along with anything the aggressive person wants to do. They enjoy the adventure and are caught up in the excitement of being in love. They will seldom express opposition to the aggressive person's ideas. When the two of them walk into a room, the aggressive person will assess what needs to be done and take charge to make it happen while the passive person stands by, perhaps talking to a friend, waiting to see what the evening will bring. The aggressive person will often engage the passive person by asking them to do something specific to move the cause along. Because they are in love with the aggressor, the passive personality often complies and may even feel good about having been a part of the process.

While there is nothing innately wrong with either of these personality traits, they do hold the potential for irritation after marriage. When the heightened emotions of being in love have faded, the passive person will be more resistant to the request of the aggressor and may feel that they are being manipulated or controlled. The aggressor may feel frustrated and even angry with the hesitation of the passive personality. It is certainly possible for these two individuals to build a successful marriage, but it requires the aggressor to be empathetic and understanding of the passive personality. He must take time to hear the concerns of the passive individual and even to realize the assets that they bring to the marriage. For example, "looking before one leaps" is always a good idea. The passive person is far more likely than the aggressor to be "looking." On the other hand, the passive person must allow the aggressive person to use her strengths and let her leap before it is too late. If you cannot conscientiously leap with her, then hold the rope while she does so. Together you will accomplish much in life, if you learn how to complement each other, rather than be competitors.

If you can discuss this personality difference before marriage and gain some experience in working together as a team, you are far more likely to make this difference an asset rather than a liability once you are married.

Professors and Dancers

Some people are extremely logical in their reasoning. They progress through rational steps and reach what to them is a logical conclusion. Other people simply know in their heart what is right in a given situation. They cannot tell you why or how they reached that conclusion; they simply know that it is the right decision.

I have sometimes called the logical thinker the *professor*. For the professor, everything must be reasoned out. "We must have logical reasons for everything we do. If it is not logical, we shouldn't do it." The intuitive person is more like the *dancer*. "We don't need logical reasons for everything we do. We do some things simply because we enjoy them. I don't know why. Do I always have to know why? I want to do it just because." Before marriage the professor was enamored with the intuitive wisdom of the dancer while the dancer was proud of the professor's logic. However, after marriage the professor is slowly driven insane by the same illogical behavior, while the dancer wonders how she can continue living with a person so obsessed with reason.

One husband said to his wife, "Trish, listen to me. The walls are not dirty; they don't need painting again. Don't you understand that?" His wife responded, "Yes, I understand that. But I don't want green walls any longer." The professor has a difficult time making decisions based on desire. The dancer cannot imagine why anyone would want to be held in the prison of logic.

These personality differences often go undiscovered and undiscussed before marriage. During the dating phase of the relationship, decisions are often made simply because he and she want to please each other. After marriage, when life gets serious and real, this desire to please each other is not as natural. When differences emerge, the logical thinker will seek to press the intuitive thinker into having logical reasons for their position. This is expecting and demanding the impossible. The intuitive person will never process life with the logic of the professor.

If you try to force each other into your own personality mold, you may spend a lifetime in conflict.

If you try to force each other into your own personality mold, you may spend a lifetime in conflict. We must recognize that logical and intuitive thinking are both legitimate ways of processing life. We must focus not on the process whereby we reach our conclusions but on finding conclusions with which both of us can agree. The principles we discussed in Chapter Four on how to resolve disagreements without arguing will be extremely helpful to couples who have this personality difference.

The Organizer and the Free Spirit

The *organizer* will give attention to the details while the *spontaneous* person—the "free spirit"—thinks, "The details will take care of themselves." Organizers are planners; they will spend months in preparation for a trip out of town. They will check three different websites, looking for the best airfare. They will make sure the rental car has GPS. They will make hotel reservations weeks in advance. They will give similar attention to where they will eat and what they will do, and certainly, they will make sure that they pack the right equipment. The spontaneous person waits until the night before the trip and says, "Why don't we go to the coast instead of the mountains? The sun is so beautiful and the weather is wonderful." This sends the organizer into a tailspin and the vacation becomes torture.

Before marriage, Beth was impressed with Trent's organizational skills. "You check your online bank balance every day? That's amazing!" However, after marriage she is asking, "You want me to write down every expense? That's impossible. No one does that." Trent, of course, quickly shows her his little notebook with every expense accurately recorded. To him, it's simply a matter of being responsible.

Trent will also load the dishwasher in a very organized manner. Plates, bowls, glasses, and silverware—all in their appropriate positions. Beth on the other hand will likely load the dishwasher like she loads the washing machine. Her objective is simply to get the door closed—the dishwasher will take care of the rest. Trent will be quick to point out the chipped plates and broken glasses that are the result of *her* whimsical attitude.

In my own marriage, it took me several years to realize that Karolyn would never load a dishwasher the way I loaded it. She simply was not wired with that ability. All of my lectures about why she should not cradle two spoons with peanut butter between them fell on deaf ears. I learned the hard way that life is more than a few chipped dishes, broken glasses, and dirty spoons. I had to give her the freedom to be who she is and, in turn, she freely relinquished the task of loading the dishwasher. If I must rush off to an evening meeting, she will gladly do the job and I will accept the results.

Trent will also pay the bills in a very organized, methodical manner. If he is out of town for a few days on a business trip, he will expect Beth to have the bills stacked neatly on his desk when he returns. However, chances are Beth will not remember what she did with the mail or even if she brought it inside the house. He may find the bills in the car, on the floor, or under the couch cushion. He is amazed that anyone could be so irresponsible. Beth is equally amazed that anyone could be so rigid. This personality difference has the potential for heated conflicts.

This personality difference can be easily observed in the dating relationship if the couple is looking for it. However, most couples are not. If the organizer sees the spontaneous personality of his dating partner, he will likely admire it and respond positively to her spontaneous ideas. If the spontaneous person sees the organizational skills of the partner, she will most certainly admire the trait and perhaps even express her appreciation. However, if the couple can be a bit more realistic and acknowledge the potential conflicts in this personality difference and discuss how they might handle such conflicts after marriage, they may save themselves the trauma of being shocked by personality clashes after marriage. The fact that you have acknowledged the potential conflicts and discussed possible solutions will make it much easier for you to discover such solutions when the inevitable conflict arises.

Because personality differences are so profound and because they strongly affect our behavior, I encourage all couples who are seriously contemplating marriage to fill out a personality profile. Few things will better prepare you for the inevitable conflicts in marriage like understanding each other's personality patterns.

There are a number of personality profiles available. One I recommend was developed in Norway and made popular in this country by numerous counselors. The profile divides people into four basic temperaments: melancholy, phlegmatic, sanguine, and choleric. You can take this profile free at the following website: www.oneishy.com/personality. If you are contemplating marriage, I would encourage each of you to take the profile separately and then discuss the results. It will give you the strengths and weaknesses of each of these temperaments. Discussing your temperaments with each other can be very enlightening.

The second profile is Couple Checkup, and will measure twenty different aspects of your relationship. It will help you celebrate your strengths and identify areas that need growth. There is a separate profile for dating couples, engaged couples, and married couples. There is a charge for this profile, but in my opinion it is an excellent investment in your relationship. You may access the profile at www.couplecheckup.com.

Taking either or both of these assessments will not only provide you with meaningful discussion, it will lead you to a deeper understanding of each other's personality patterns. Understanding personality will make it much easier for you to accept the behavior of the other person in a given situation.

If the two of you go for premarital counseling, your counselor may also suggest an assessment tool called PREPARE/ENRICH. This is a more comprehensive profile and is geared specifically to couples who are thinking of marriage. This profile will need to be administered, scored, and interpreted by a counselor, but it can be an extremely helpful exercise as a couple moves toward marriage.[1]

Talking It Over

1. On a scale of 1–10, rate yourself on the following personality traits. 10 means extremely high and 1 means extremely low.

a. Optimistic
b. Pessimistic

c. Neat
d. Messy

e. Babbling Brook
f. Dead Sea

g. Pointer
h. Painter

i. Aggressive
j. Passive

k. Logical
l. Intuitive

m. Organizer
n. Spontaneous

2. Encourage your dating partner to do the above exercise and then discuss your answers with each other, giving illustrations as to why you rated yourself a particular score.

3. If you are seriously considering marriage, perhaps you would like to take one or both of the free personality profiles discussed in this chapter. They can be found at the following websites: oneishy.com/personality and couplecheckup.com.

4. If you receive premarital counseling from a counselor or religious leader, you may ask them about the possibility of taking the PREPARE/ENRICH assessment.

Epilogue

In this book, I have shared with you what I wish someone had told me before I got married. If Karolyn and I had discussed the issues I have raised on these pages, our first years of marriage would have been much easier. Since we did not discuss these issues, our marriage was filled with conflicts, misunderstandings, and frustration. I know the feeling of being married and miserable; of thinking, "I've married the wrong woman." I reasoned that surely if I had married the "right one," it would not be this difficult.

Yes, we eventually found answers to our frustrations and resolution to our conflicts. We learned how to listen to each other empathetically and understand feelings and desires and to reach workable solutions. For many years we have had a loving, supportive, satisfying marital relationship and have invested our lives in helping other couples discover the same. It is my desire that this book will help thousands of couples have that kind of marriage, without the years of pain and struggle we experienced.

If you are single and not currently involved in a dating relationship, I hope the ideas of this book will be tucked away in your mind for future reference. You now have a more realistic idea of what needs to be considered before you make the decision to get married. When you begin to feel the "tingles" for someone, I hope that you will take this book off the shelf and let it be a guide in developing a healthy dating relationship and a wise decision on whether or not to say, "I do!"

For those of you who are in a committed dating relationship, I hope that this book will be your trusted companion as you get to know each other better. I encourage you to discuss the topics openly and honestly, and seek to be realistic about what you discover. If so, I believe you will make a wise decision about whether or not you should get married.

For those who are already officially or unofficially "engaged," I hope that you will dig deeply into the issues I have raised. I encourage you not simply to read the chapters but to answer the questions and follow the suggestions I have made at the end of each chapter. Some of you may discover that your engagement is premature; that you really did not know each other well enough to make that decision. If so, I hope you will have the courage to be honest with each other, accept the embarrassment this may bring, and either postpone or break your engagement. I assure you that a broken engagement, while painful, is not nearly as painful as a divorce three years later.

If, on the other hand, you conclude that you hold enough in

common to build a successful marriage, then your discussion of these issues will better prepare you to make that dream a reality. I genuinely believe that if couples will thoroughly discuss the content of this book, they will enter marriage with a much more realistic view of how to have a successful marriage.

A few years ago, a survey revealed that 87 percent of single adults between the ages of twenty and thirty affirmed, "I want to have one marriage that will last for a lifetime."[1] They have seen their parents divorce and felt the pain of abandonment. That is not what they desire to replicate. The tragedy is that many of them have no idea how to reach the aspiration of a lifelong positive marriage relationship. It is my desire that this book will provide them with that information.

If you have found this book helpful, I hope that you will recommend it to your friends. I welcome your feedback and suggestions at www.5lovelanguages.com.

Appendix

Developing a **HEALTHY DATING** *Relationship*

In Western culture, marriage is typically preceded by a period of dating. In its broadest sense, a date is an appointment between a male and female who agree to spend a segment of time together for the purpose of getting better acquainted. There are two distinct stages of dating. The first is casual dating. Casual dating may or may not have romantic overtones. It may simply be two symphony devotees agreeing to attend the performance together and perhaps have dinner or dessert afterwards. Or it could be two cyclists who agree to do a twenty-mile ride together on Saturday. If there is no romantic interest and no such interest develops after a period of casual dating, the couple will probably consider themselves friends and not think of their relationship as a dating relationship.

Casual dating relationships are often accompanied by a romantic interest on the part of one or both individuals. However, the couple may have numerous dates without acknowledging this interest. The focus of casual dating is enjoying life together and sharing a common interest. Casual dating is typically nonexclusive; that is, one or both of the individuals may also have dating relationships with other people. While the one with strong romantic feelings may be emotionally hurt knowing that the other person is dating someone else, they are not likely to verbalize their hurt because they know that no commitment has been made.

Casual dating normally moves in one of three directions. If no romantic interest develops and they each have a strong common interest, they may develop a strong friendship that focuses on some common activity. These kinds of mutually enjoyable relationships often continue for years.

A second possibility is that the casual dating relationship will end. Perhaps one of them has a strong romantic attraction and the other does not. This in itself may become a conflict that leads to ending the relationship. Or, if neither has a romantic interest in the other and they have no strong mutual bond, the relationship dies a natural death.

The third possibility is that in time, even if it were not present in the beginning, they each develop a strong romantic interest in the other. Their times together are mutually enjoyable, and they begin to think that they may be "falling in love" with each other. The relationship will move from casual dating to committed dating.

Committed dating is much more serious than casual dating. It is normally perceived as an exclusive relationship. If one of them chooses to date someone else, the one who is betrayed will experience great pain. They will not hesitate to verbalize their pain, and the ensuing conversation will lead either to the breakup of the relationship or to a commitment to each other. It is this committed stage of dating that I wish to discuss in this appendix. I believe that developing a healthy dating relationship is the best preparation for a healthy marriage. I am not suggesting that all such dating couples will end up marrying each other. I am suggesting that a healthy dating relationship will enable them to answer the question "To marry or not to marry?" more wisely. Therefore, let's turn our attention to those factors that characterize this type of dating relationship.

Healthy dating relationships will focus on "getting to know" each other. This is really what serious dating is all about. The human psyche is a complex combination of heredity and environment. What you see on the outside is not necessarily what you will discover on the inside. This process of discovery requires a high level of honesty on the part of both individuals. In the early stages of dating, we tend to "put our best foot forward." That is, we strive to make a good impression. But that is not the attitude which leads to a healthy dating relationship.

Every individual has a unique history. That history has brought you to where you are today. We cannot know each other without sharing our histories. This means that we must be willing to share our failures as well as our successes. One young man said to me in the counseling office, "I'm afraid to tell her that I was in a youth detention facility for three months for shoplifting when I was sixteen years old. I'm afraid if she knows that, she will stop dating me." "How long do you wish to hide this information?" I asked. "Until you are engaged or until you are married?"

"I guess that wouldn't be fair, would it?" he responded.

To build a relationship upon deception or hidden truth is to sabotage the relationship. By nature, we are quick to share our successes, for they make us look good. We are more hesitant to share our failures because even we are hurt by the memories. Yet healthy dating relationships are built upon truth.

There are two areas in which honesty is often extremely difficult. One is in sharing our sexual history and the other is in sharing our financial history. However, I strongly urge couples in a serious dating relationship to reveal these areas of life. Part of my motivation in encouraging them to do so is that these are the two areas that often cause the most conflict in marriage. To enter marriage without revealing these two aspects of who we are is unfair to our partner and to ourselves.

Recently a young lady said to me, "My dating partner has shared with me that he has been sexually active with three other girls over the past eight years. I must confess I found this very difficult to deal with. In fact, I'm still trying to deal with it, but I'm so grateful that he shared the truth with me. Had I found it out after we were engaged or married, I think I would have felt betrayed." I think she was exactly right and he was extremely wise in sharing the truth. Simply because something is "hard to deal with" does not mean it should be ignored. Real life has to do with dealing with hard issues. Learning how to do this while dating prepares you for a healthy marriage in the future.

What about finances? Sharing financial information may be difficult but is also necessary in a healthy dating relationship, especially if that relationship seems to be moving toward an engagement and marriage. Sharing with each other how you manage your money will likely lead you to the discovery that you have different patterns of saving, giving, and spending. Negotiating these differences before marriage will make the transition into marriage much easier. For example, if one of you regularly gives 10 percent of your income to charitable causes and the other gives 2 percent or nothing, this difference has the potential of strong marital conflict if not resolved before marriage.

The amount of debt and the type of debt certainly needs to be revealed to each other. How much money you have in savings and the purpose of your savings account also is important information. When one of you tends to be a *saver* and the other a *spender*, negotiation is in order. Negotiation involves discussing the matter fully and finding a solution that is acceptable to both of you. These are not matters that would ever be discussed while you are in the casual stage of dating, but when you move to the committed stage, and especially when you start thinking about engagement and marriage, these are extremely important matters.

Dating also allows you to get to know each other's family dynamics. How do her mom and dad relate to each other? And what about his parents? How do they relate to each other and what kind of relationship does he have with his dad and mom? Are parents divorced in either family? What is the nature of the present relationship each of you has with your parents? You should make great effort to spend time with the family of your dating partner. If you should eventually get married, they will be a part of your life for a long time.

In a healthy dating relationship, you will each foster the educational and vocational goals of the other. After all, our education and vocation are a huge part of life. The young man who says to his girlfriend who is a junior in college, "Why don't you drop out of college and marry me? I'm going to have a career in the military and you don't need a college degree," is not the kind of young man who is ready for marriage. This attitude reveals his own self-centeredness. In a mature relationship, we are encouraging each other and helping each other in the pursuit of educational and vocational goals.

A healthy dating relationship will also be a balanced relationship. In an effort to identify the various aspects of our humanity, we often use such words as *intellectual, emotional, social, spiritual*, and *physical*. While in reality these five can never be isolated, because they are intertwined, it is helpful to focus on these five areas during the dating relationship.

The *intellectual* has to do with our thoughts, our desires, and our perceptions of life. We often speak of intellectual compatibility. The question is "Do we have the ability to share our reactions to a newspaper or magazine article and to stimulate thought without condemning or arguing with each other?" If our political ideas clash, how do we process our differences? Learning how to disagree and not be disagreeable is one of the evidences of intellectual compatibility. If a man who seldom reads a book is dating a woman who is a voracious reader, the question is, do they have the foundation for intellectual compatibility? The one who makes straight A's in college may have great difficulty communicating with the person who squeaked by with C's and D+'s. Intellectually are you close enough to hold hands? Do your conversations about intellectual matters stimulate growth or condemnation?

The *emotional* aspect of life has to do with our unsolicited emotional responses to the events we encounter in life. Some people hear the siren of a fire truck and are gripped with fear. Another may observe someone crying and feel extremely uncomfortable. Our feelings are not something we choose; they simply come as a part of life. Learning to share these emotions and understand where they are coming from, and choosing a positive response to our feelings are an important part of the process of maturing. Learning how to help each other process emotions is a part of growing a healthy dating relationship.

We are also *social* creatures. We seek to share life with others. There is something about human nature that desires to live in community. That is why one of the most stringent of punishments is "solitary confinement." However, there is great variance in how, when, and where we like to spend time with people. Social events are abundant in our society. Thousands of people every week spend time in stadiums, watching various sporting events, while others are gathered in symphony halls, theaters, and churches. All of these are social events but the same people do not necessarily attend all of those events. What are your social interests? What are those of your dating partner? One young lady said to me, "I find it really hard to understand how he could sit in the stands all day Sunday and watch cars run around in a circle. If that is his idea of a social event, I don't know that we are living on the same planet." She may well be right. The good thing is that she is discovering this while they are in the dating stage and not after they are married.

Then there is the *spiritual* aspect of life. I mentioned earlier that my academic field is the study of anthropology, which is a study of human cultures. We have never discovered a culture in which people do not have beliefs about the nonmaterial world. Man seems inescapably spiritual. So, what are your concepts of spiritual reality and what are the perceptions of your dating partner? How fully have you discussed this area of life? Because spiritual beliefs often affect the rest of life, this aspect of life is exceedingly important. One lady said to me, "I don't know if I am going to be able to continue in this relationship. I am a Wiccan and my boyfriend is a Christian. Every time we talk about it, we get into an argument. I like him a lot and I enjoy being with him. But I'm not sure our relationship can survive our differences in spiritual perceptions." I commended her for being mature enough to face this reality.

The fifth dimension of our humanity is that we are *physical creatures*. This is the most tangible and visible part of us. Often it was physical attraction that initiated our relationship in the first place. We were both "attracted" to each other physically. Affirming physical touch is a part of almost all dating relationships. People differ widely on what they believe to be appropriate touches in a dating relationship. What is important in a healthy relationship is that we respect each other's boundaries. To force a dating partner to go beyond these boundaries is never an act of love and will be detrimental to the relationship.

Unfortunately in contemporary society, the misguided emphasis on sexuality has made it difficult for many couples to have a balanced dating relationship. The current phenomenon of "hooking up," in which couples have sex on the first date and their relationship is focused on the sexual experience, fails to qualify either as dating or a relationship. Such encounters either grow out of or lead to sexual addiction, which is certainly not a foundation upon which to build a marriage.

Balancing the intellectual, emotional, social, spiritual, and physical aspects of life is one of the characteristics of a healthy dating relationship. If you are in a serious dating relationship, let me encourage you to use the learning exercises at the end of this appendix to stimulate your thoughts in developing a healthy dating relationship.

Learning Exercises

1. Since getting to know each other is one of the primary purposes of a serious dating relationship, use the following questions to stimulate conversation.
    - *What personal accomplishments have we shared with each other?*
    - *What personal failures have we shared and what remains to be shared?*
    - *To what degree have we shared our sexual history with each other?*
    - *What do we know about each other's financial history?*
2. Since your extended family has influenced each of you greatly, use the following questions to help develop understanding of these relationships.
    - *How would you describe the marital relationship of your mom and dad?*
    - *From your perspective, what was your parents' main philosophy on child rearing? How do you agree or disagree with their approach to parenting?*
    - *What kind of relationship do you presently have with your father?*
    - *What is the nature of your relationship with your mother?*
    - *If and when you get married, in what way would you like for your marriage to be different from that of your parents?*
3. Since educational and vocational accomplishments are a big part of life, use the following questions to explore this aspect of life.
    - *What are your educational goals for the next five years?*

- *From what you know about your interests, what vocational goals do you presently have?*
- *Has your dating relationship been an asset or a liability to reaching these goals? In what way?*
- *To what degree do you feel your dating partner accepts and appreciates your goals?*

4. Since a healthy dating relationship is a balanced relationship, use the following questions to identify areas that may need further development.

A. Intellectual

1) *Have you taken time to compare your college or high school grades?*
2) *Have you ever read a magazine or online article and discussed your perceptions of the validity of the article?*
3) *What television programs do you typically watch? How often do you discuss your reactions to the programs that you view?*
4) *When you share your opinion on political issues, how does your dating partner typically respond?*
5) *When you have disagreements, to what degree do you feel free to share your perspective? How do you typically respond when your partner shares his/her perspective?*
6) *Have you learned to disagree without being disagreeable?*

B. Emotional

1) *What emotions have you felt throughout this day? What stimulated those emotions?*
2) *How often, and to what degree, do you share your emotions with each other?*

3) *When you do share emotions, how does the other person typically respond? What improvements would you like to see in this part of your relationship?*

C. Social

1) *What social events have the two of you attended together in the last month? Share with each other your level of enjoyment or frustration with these events.*
2) *What sports event do you most enjoy attending or watching on television?*
3) *Do either of you have interest in attending musical events? Have you discussed how this interest affects your relationship?*
4) *How many movies have you watched together in the past six weeks? Did you discuss the content of these movies afterwards?*
5) *When you attend social events that involve talking with other people, what bothers you most about your partner's behavior?*
6) *What improvements would you like to see in this part of your relationship?*

D. Spiritual

1) *Have the two of you discussed your spiritual backgrounds?*
2) *If you grew up in a religious home, have you embraced the faith of your childhood? Or have you rejected it? Or are you still trying to decide? What is your view of God?*
3) *If you have children, will you raise them in a particular faith?*
4) *What changes would you like to see in this part of your relationship?*

E. Physical

1) *What kind of affirming touches communicate love to you?*
2) *Have you discussed with each other what you think are inappropriate touches?*
3) *To what degree have you felt pressured to accept touches that you feel are inappropriate?*
4) *What changes would you like to see in this aspect of your relationship?*

Notes

CHAPTER ONE

That being in love is not an adequate foundation for building a successful marriage

1. Dorothy Tennov, *Love and Limerence* (New York: Stein and Day, 1972), 142.

CHAPTER THREE

That the saying "Like mother, like daughter" or "Like father, like son" is not a myth

1. James Garbarino, *Lost Boys: Why Our Sons Turn Violent and How We Can Save Them* (New York: Free Press, 1999), 50.
2. Theodore Jacob and Sheri Johnson, "Parenting Influences on the Development of Alcohol Abuse and Dependence." *Alcohol Health and Research World*, vol. 21, no. 3 (1997): 204–209. For additional information, see the National Association for Children of Alcoholics website: www.nacoa.net/impfacts.htm.

CHAPTER FIVE

That apologizing is a sign of strength

1. 1 John 1:8–9.

2. Gary D. Chapman and Jennifer Thomas, *The Five Languages of Apology: How to Experience Healing in All Your Relationships* (Chicago: Northfield Publishing, 2006), 125–28.

CHAPTER SIX

That forgiveness is not a feeling

1. Psalm 103:12.

CHAPTER EIGHT

That we needed a plan for handling our money

1. Acts 20:35.
2. Ellie Kay, *The Little Book of Big Savings* (Colorado Springs: WaterBrook Press, 2009).

CHAPTER NINE

That mutual sexual fulfillment is not automatic

1. Deuteronomy 24:5.
2. See William G. Axinn and Arland Thorton, "The Relationship Between Cohabitation and Divorce: Selectivity or casual influence?" *Demography* 29 (1992): 357–74; and Zheng Wu, "Premarital Cohabitation and Postmarital Cohabitation Union Formation," *Journal of Family Issues* 16 (1995): 212–32.
3. Barbara Wilson, *The Invisible Bond: How to Break Free from Your Sexual Past* (Colorado Springs: Multnomah Publishers, 2006).
4. Clifford and Joyce Penner, *The Gift of Sex* (Nashville: W Publishing Group, 2003).

CHAPTER TEN

That I was marrying into a family

1. Psalm 133:1.
2. Ron L. Deal, *The Smart Step-Family* (Minneapolis: Bethany House, 2002).

CHAPTER ELEVEN

That spirituality is not to be equated with "going to church"

1. 2 Corinthians 6:14–16.
2. Genesis 1:1.
3. Genesis 1:27 (TNIV).
4. Hebrews 1:1–3.

CHAPTER TWELVE

That personality profoundly influences behavior

1. For more information, or to locate a counselor in your area, visit: www.prepare-enrich.com.

EPILOGUE

1. Kim McAlister, "The X-Generation," *HR Magazine* 39 (May 1994): 21.

Resources

Websites

Startmarriageright.com. Articles, videos, and the latest resources to help you have a successful marriage because your wedding day is just the beginning!

Dr. Gary Chapman: www.5lovelanguages.com. Numerous resources to help you discover the marriage you've always wanted.

FamilyLife: www.familylife.com. A variety of marriage resources.

Marriage Partnership: www.marriagepartnership.com. Articles and insights geared to couples in the early years.

Financial expert Dave Ramsey: www.daveramsey.com. Includes many resources specifically for young couples.

Crown Financial Ministries: www.crown.org. A variety of helpful financial tools. Excellent for those starting out.

Ron Deal: www.successfulstepfamilies.com. Excellent resources for couples contemplating remarriage after divorce or the death of a spouse.

Books

Ron L. Deal, *The Smart Step Family* (Bethany House). Seven steps to a healthy step-up family.

Ron L. Deal and David H. Olson, *The Remarriage Checkup* (Bethany House). Advice for couples who are contemplating remarriage after divorce or the death of a spouse.

Tim and Joy Downs, *One of Us Must Be Crazy... and I'm Pretty Sure It's You* and *Fight Fair!* (Moody). Advice on dealing with conflict.

Emerson Eggerichs, *Love & Respect* (Integrity). What wives and husbands really want.

Tony Evans, *For Married Men Only* and *For Married Women Only* (Moody). Biblical insights.

Jerry B. Jenkins, *Hedges* (Crossway). On protecting your marriage from infidelity.

Kevin Leman, *Sheet Music* (Tyndale). On sexual intimacy.

Clifford and Joyce Penner, *The Gift of Sex* (W Publishing Group). A forthright, sensitive guide to understanding sexuality.

Greg Smalley and Erin Smalley, *Before You Plan Your Wedding . . . Plan Your Marriage* (Howard). Insights from a younger married couple.

John Townsend and Henry Cloud, *Boundaries in Marriage* (Zondervan). Dealing with some of the psychological issues.

Ed Young, *The Ten Commandments of Marriage* (Moody). Counsel from a well-known pastor.

Log on to

5lovelanguages.com

- discover your love language
- explore other resources
- get free stuff
- locate events
- listen to podcasts
- share your love story
- and more!

We want to help you feel loved.

5lovelanguages.com

The 5 Love Languages™

by Dr. Gary Chapman

The 5 Love Languages™ Men's Edition

A relationship book from a man's perspective is a big plus. Discovering that the key to interpreting your wife's feelings isn't a gender issue? That's an even bigger breakthrough. Turn evocative marital issues into manageable, practical action points.

The 5 Love Languages™

What if you could say or do just the right thing guaranteed to make that special someone feel loved? The secret is learning the right love language! Millions of couples have learned the simple way to express their feelings and bring joy back into marriage.

The 5 Love Languages™ Gift Edition

The perfect gift for an engagement, wedding, or anniversary! Give the happy couple the secret to finding true happiness in marriage—the key is learning the right love language! This beautiful new gift edition will be a treasured resource.

5lovelanguages.com

AVAILABLE AT YOUR FAVORITE LOCAL OR ONLINE BOOKSTORE

Attend a conference

by Dr. Gary Chapman

Join Gary . . . at *The Marriage You've Always Wanted* conference in your area—check 5lovelanguages.com for details.

The Marriage You've Always Wanted

Dr. Gary Chapman has helped millions of couples toward true unity and oneness. With his unique brand of humor, insight, groundbreaking revelations and straightforward common sense, he can help you build *The Marriage You've Always Wanted*, too. From the deeply emotional to the gritty and practical, you'll find answers you can use to grow today.

The Marriage You've Always Wanted Bible Study

Learn how to share yourself fully with your spouse and express love in a meaningful way. By sharing this resource, couples will discuss and reflect on such areas as money, anger, forgiveness, and spirituality, all in an easy-to-use workbook format. Ideal for personal and group study.

5lovelanguages.com

AVAILABLE AT YOUR FAVORITE LOCAL OR ONLINE BOOKSTORE

Learn how to resolve conflict

ISBN-13: 978-1-881273-79-0

ISBN-13: 978-1-881273-88-2

The Five Languages of Apology

We are experts at wronging each other, but when it comes to setting things right, we all could use some help. Counselor Jennifer Thomas joins Dr. Chapman in an eye-opening study of one of the most important yet least understood pillars of human relationships: the apology. Surprisingly, saying "I'm sorry" isn't primarily a matter of will—it's a matter of how.

Anger: Handling a Powerful Emotion in a Healthy Way

When anger explodes out of control, it can cause irreparable damage; buried, unresolved anger can be just as destructive. How can we handle our anger—and help those we love with theirs? Relationship expert Gary Chapman reveals some surprising insights and techniques for managing anger in a healthy, even productive way.

5lovelanguages.com

AVAILABLE AT YOUR FAVORITE LOCAL OR ONLINE BOOKSTORE

Strengthen your finances strengthen your relationship

Debt-Free Living

With people's credit, mortgages, car payments, salaries, commissions, and bills fluctuating daily, *Debt-Free Living* has never looked more attractive. Learn about the origin of most financial troubles and break out of the debt cycle. *Debt-Free Living* is a necessary resource to battle the ever-present temptation and trappings of more and more debt that keeps weighing you down.

Money and Marriage God's Way

Financial woes and marriage troubles can rob couples of precious opportunities to savor the blessings of companionship, family, and peace that God intends for His people. *Money and Marriage God's Way* will help you discover God's approach to growing your finances and strengthening your relationship with your mate. It highlights key issues like debt, conflict, spending, investing, saving, and budgeting.

moodypublishers.com

AVAILABLE AT YOUR FAVORITE LOCAL OR ONLINE BOOKSTORE

There is hope

True intimacy is available

Undefiled: Redemption from Sexual Sin, Restoration for Broken Relationships

When practiced as God intends, spirituality and sexuality both draw us closer to Christ. Spiritual maturity and sexual maturity go hand-in-hand, and together they hold out the promise of redemption and restoration needed by everyone who has been damaged by sexual sin. There is hope. Real change is possible; true intimacy is available. To the person who has failed time and time again sexually, God's message is simple: you, too, can be *Undefiled*.

moodypublishers.com

AVAILABLE AT YOUR FAVORITE LOCAL OR ONLINE BOOKSTORE